Fighting for Spain

Fighting for Spain

The International Brigades in the Civil War, 1936–1939

Alexander Clifford

Pen & Sword
MILITARY

First published in Great Britain in 2020 by
PEN & SWORD MILITARY
An imprint of Pen & Sword Books Ltd
Yorkshire – Philadelphia

ISBN 978-1-52677-438-5

Typeset by Concept, Huddersfield, West Yorkshire, HD4 5JL
Printed and bound by TJ International Ltd

Pen & Sword Books Ltd incorporates the Imprints of Aviation, Atlas,
Family History, Fiction, Maritime, Military, Discovery, Politics, History,
Archaeology, Select, Wharncliffe Local History, Wharncliffe True Crime,
Military Classics, Wharncliffe Transport, Leo Cooper, The Praetorian Press,
Remember When, White Owl, Seaforth Publishing and Frontline Publishing.

For a complete list of Pen & Sword titles please contact
PEN & SWORD BOOKS LTD
47 Church Street, Barnsley, South Yorkshire, S70 2AS, England
E-mail: enquiries@pen-and-sword.co.uk
Website: www.pen-and-sword.co.uk
or
PEN & SWORD BOOKS
1950 Lawrence Rd, Havertown, PA 19083, USA
E-mail: uspen-and-sword@casematepublishers.com
Website: www.penandswordbooks.com

Contents

Dedication

For Peter Anderson, to whom I owe
the enormous debt of igniting
a livelong passion.

Acknowledgements

I wish to thank my friends and family, most of all my partner Róisín, my brother Freddy (who has written the profiles on weapons included in this volume) and my parents, for all the help and support they have given me over the last couple of years in researching and writing this book. My research into the civil war would have been impossible without my friend Jose Del Pino, whose translation skills have made up for my own linguistical deficiencies. Finally, I must pay tribute to Pen & Sword and especially to Rupert Harding for doing so much to shape this project, Dom West for drawing the fantastic military maps commissioned for the book and Sarah Cook, my editor, who has quite simply worked wonders!

All images used in this book are public domain images sourced from Wikimedia Commons, unless otherwise stated in the caption. The author would like to thank the Imperial War Museum, German Bundesarchiv and Magnum Photos for use of their collections. For those images which are reproduced under Creative Commons Share Alike licences, the full licence can be found at the web addresses below.

Disclaimer: While every effort has been made to trace copyright holders, if any have inadvertently been overlooked, please contact the publishers, who will be pleased to acknowledge them in future editions of the work.

Creative Commons licences can be viewed in full at:

CC BY-SA 4.0:
https://creativecommons.org/licenses/by-sa/4.0/legalcode

CC BY-SA 3.0 DE:
https://creativecommons.org/licenses/by-sa/3.0/de/legalcode

CC BY-SA 3.0:
https://creativecommons.org/licenses/by-sa/3.0/legalcode

CC BY 2.5:
https://creativecommons.org/licenses/by/2.5/legalcode

CC BY 2.0:
https://creativecommons.org/licenses/by/2.0/legalcode

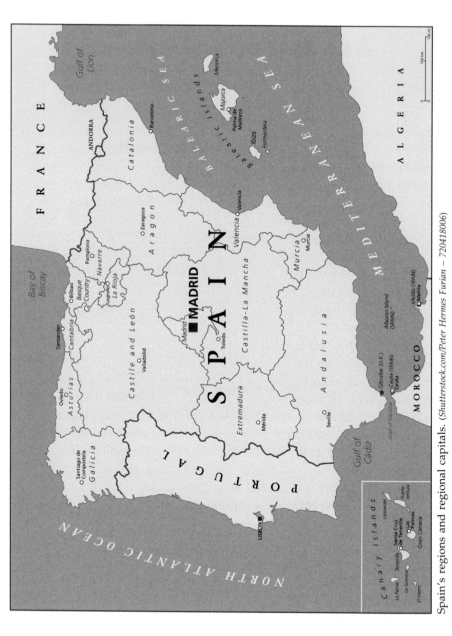

Spain's regions and regional capitals. (*Shutterstock.com/Peter Hermes Furian – 720418006*)

Introduction

Spain's Civil War

In July 1936 Rebel generals launched a coup against the left-wing elected government of the Spanish Republic. Eventually coming to be led by General Francisco Franco, the Rebels, who labelled themselves Nationalists, but were widely referred to as Fascists, soon found that their coup had failed, serving only to split the nation into two rival zones, one insurgent, the other Loyalist. Over the next three years the two factions, driven by ideological idealism and hatred, fought one of Europe's bloodiest civil wars. Foreign intervention was to prove crucial in the outcome of the struggle, with Franco gaining support from Hitler and Mussolini less than a fortnight into the conflict and Soviet aid to the Republicans arriving some months later.

In the English-speaking world, the Spanish Civil War is perhaps best remembered through the exploits of thousands of foreign volunteers from across the globe who joined the International Brigades – a Comintern-organised force of Communists, Socialists and others who took their opposition to fascism to extraordinary lengths. Their passionate political commitment to Spain's cause and their determination in battle led to them becoming the crack troops of the Republic's newly built People's Army, time and again at the tip of the spear, fighting in the toughest spots. Although never totalling many more than 15,000 men in an army that eventually exceeded 800,000, a confidential Soviet report on the state of the Brigades at one of their lowest ebbs in terms of numbers and morale described them as representing a quarter of the Republic's shock troops – troops the Republic simply could not do without. The reason for this was that a high proportion of the men in the ranks of the International Brigades were 'commissar material', ideologically devoted to the cause, unlike many of the People's Army's reluctant conscripts and unreliable militiamen. However, the story of the Brigades is one of idealism and incompetence in equal measure; the leadership, tactics and firepower of

Francisco Franco, Europe's youngest general, hero of the Rif War, Nationalist Generalissimo, Caudillo (leader) of Spain for life after his victory in the civil war.

Territorial division of Spain at the outbreak of civil war in July 1936. Republican-held territory is dark, Nationalist light. (*Wikimedia User Nordnordwest, CC BY-SA 3.0*)

the Internationalists were often found wanting and their fighting spirit was worn away by frequent military disasters. Reportedly a staggering 93 per cent of the Brigaders would become casualties if minor injuries are counted alongside killed, wounded, missing and captured – virtually every volunteer who survived the war had suffered at least a minor wound in the countless bloody combats the Internationals fought.

The Spanish Civil War is a complex conflict that can be best understood in the wider European context of the rise of fascism in an age of ideological extremes. Spain was a backwards nation by Western standards, with high levels of illiteracy and relatively little industry and infrastructure. Poverty, especially in the rural south, was extreme and the social divisions between landowners and peasants, employers and unions, Catholics and anti-clericals were almost impossible to bridge. Additionally, Spain had entirely lost the world empire which once marked it out as a great power, save a small protectorate in northern Morocco, just across the Straits of Gibraltar. A long and bitter colonial war fought in the

Moroccan Rif from 1909 to 1926 only served to highlight Spanish weakness, with victory not coming until French intervention in the conflict. Amidst a wave of optimism, a new political system emerged from a bloodless revolution in the spring of 1931 with the foundation of the Spanish Second Republic – Spain's first true democracy, at least in the modern sense of the term. A coalition of Republicans (liberal, middle-class parties) and the Socialist labour movement drafted a new constitution which promised democratic rights and greater economic equality. However, it was immediately seen as a partisan document by much of the political right, while many of the left felt the pace of change was too slow. The new government clearly made mistakes in directly challenging the power and position of the Catholic Church and army, serving only to stoke passions and unite the opposition. Tensions rose further as rebellions by right-wingers in the army and far-left Anarchists were defeated

Scene from the Annual disaster, a humiliating defeat for the Spanish in the Rif War. The bitter conflict in Morocco created a brutalised, proto-fascist culture in the Spanish army.

Celebrations in Barcelona at the declaration of the Republic, April 1931.
(*Bundesarchiv CC BY-SA 3.0 DE*)

and Catalonia was granted autonomy, anathema to Spanish Nationalists. Eventually, the coalition of Socialists and Republicans who had created the new system fell apart over the frustrations of office, with many on the left losing faith in the democratic project, given the intractable opposition of landowners and bosses to reforms such as land redistribution. As a result, Rightists took control of parliament in the elections of 1933 and began to turn back the Republican tide, undoing the previous government's work.

Across Europe, right-wing dictatorships had seized power, often dismantling democratic institutions from the inside, as had happened in Italy, Germany, neighbouring Portugal and, most recently, Austria. The Spanish left feared sharing the same fate as their continental comrades and was determined not to go down without a fight. Furthermore, the commitment to democracy of some Leftists was weakened by the failure of the first Republican government to deliver real progress. Meanwhile, some on the right sought to emulate the likes of Hitler and Dollfus and take control of the Republic at the ballot box before tearing down democracy and creating a corporative dictatorship. A revolutionary general strike, which came to be known as the Asturias Rising, was staged by the Socialists in 1934 but was easily crushed by the right-wing government with thousands of deaths and tens of thousands of arrests. Attitudes were hardening on both sides of the political divide, and the elections of February 1936 were contested in a febrile, win-or-die atmosphere. An electoral alliance of Leftists and Liberals known as the Popular Front won power, but the resulting government was weak, composed only of Republicans, with the Socialist Party refusing to join the coalition cabinet after earlier bitter experiences. Right-wing army officers began plotting a coup almost immediately, with an inept administration in Madrid failing to take action against the conspirators. Political violence, strikes and assassinations rocked Spain for several months as left and right polarised further and common ground became non-existent. For the right, the activities of the left, such as land seizures and strike waves, were seen as evidence of imminent Bolshevik revolution, despite the lack of a strong Communist Party in Spain. On the left, some leaders talked of the coming revolution but did nothing to bring it about, instead waiting for the rumoured military coup as the trigger for working-class action. On 17 July 1936 the officers made their move.

However, the failure of the coup to seize complete control quickly resulted in a civil war developing. The Rebel army units, supported by

Religious Spain – Nationalist soldiers observe a field mass with chaplain before battle. (*Bundesarchiv*)

Anti-clerical Spain – one of the biggest social divides was religion. Here anarchist militiamen pose in stolen priests' cassocks during the social revolution unleashed by the civil war. (*Bundesarchiv*)

rightist Spain, held large swathes of the north as well as the Moroccan protectorate, while Loyalist militias, army and police units retained control over the east, centre and most of the south, as well as a thin northern strip along the Cantabrian coast. General Franco was in Morocco at the head of the elite colonial Army of Africa, the best trained and equipped force in the Spanish army and key to Nationalist hopes of victory. However, the Navy had remained loyal to the government and so Franco's 30,000 men were trapped in the protectorate. The Generalissimo quickly sent emissaries to Rome and Berlin, and within days German and Italian aircraft were ferrying Rebel troops to mainland Spain. Hitler and Mussolini had both ideological and strategic motives in supporting the Spanish insurgents, sharing their right-wing, anti-Communist beliefs but also seeing potential benefits for themselves: Hitler intended to exploit Spanish mineral resources for his own rearmament programme while Mussolini hoped to extend his influence over the Mediterranean.

Meanwhile, the Republic stood alone. The French government had been sympathetic, but pressure from Britain and domestic opinion prevented any serious intervention. The British and Americans were indifferent, with the capitalist West flooded by horror stories of revolution and Red Terror in the Republican zone. Indeed, the civil war sparked off a genuine social revolution in the Republic, with armed militias of workers and peasants seizing control at a local level, leaving the government (lacking the repressive power of the military) powerless for a time. Eventually, the revolution would be reined in by central government and capitalist normality largely restored, but the initial seizure and collectivising of property and murder of Rightists in Republican Spain resulted in a flight of capital and ruined any chances that the Loyalists had of winning support from the Western democratic powers. The Soviet Union had expressed moral support and began fundraising for the Republic but for a time failed to intervene, Stalin being more interested in pursuing friendship with Great Britain and France than sponsoring a foreign revolution. Instead, the Soviets joined all the major powers (including Germany and Italy) in signing a Non-Intervention Agreement in August 1936, forbidding the sale of arms to either side. But by September 1936 this stance had changed dramatically. With support from the Axis powers, who flagrantly violated the Non-Intervention Agreement without rebuke from the appeasers in Britain and France, Franco's forces had achieved a rapid and bloody advance across southern Spain and were closing on Madrid. Denied the opportunity to buy arms or military supplies of any kind by the international community, the Republicans were in headlong retreat. Given that France was at that time the only ally of an otherwise diplomatically isolated Stalin, the

Soviet aid to the Republic: T-26 tanks on the left (a total of 281 were supplied to the Republicans) and BA armoured cars on the right.

Soviet dictator feared a fascist puppet of Hitler and Mussolini appearing on his ally's southern border. As has already been made clear, the Soviets were not interested in spreading revolution to Spain; in fact once they became involved, they worked consistently to rein in and indeed crush revolution and radicalism and restore capitalist order. The party line was that Spain's civil war was a fight for democracy, not for Communism or Socialism, in the vain hope that the Western powers would not be frightened off (hence Orwell's condemnation of Communist betrayal of the revolution in his novel *Homage to Catalonia*).

Soviet intervention in Spain took a number of forms. Hundreds of military and political advisers arrived to assist the Republican government and help create a new regular army, the so-called People's Army that was rapidly forged from the myriad political militias. Modern tanks and aircraft arrived to equip this new army and take on the Nationalists and their fascist backers and redress the technological imbalance. On the other hand, badly outdated small arms and artillery were also offloaded on the desperate Republic. Thanks to Soviet advice, money and the prestige brought about by Russian aid, the Spanish Communist Party grew rapidly in size and influence, although it never gained hegemony over the fragmented Spanish left, divided between the Socialists, Anarchists, Communists, Catalanists, semi-Trotskyist POUM [Workers' Marxist Unity

Axis intervention: Nazi Condor Legion Ju 87 Stuka dive-bombers in action.

Party] and liberal Republican parties. Given that, unlike Italy, the USSR was not willing to send ground troops, the Comintern (Communist International) was tasked with forming an International Brigade, a unit of 5,000 foreign volunteers who would bolster the Republican ranks and serve as a martial representation of global class solidarity, an idea that likely amounted to little more than a propaganda stunt. Thousands of left-wing volunteers had already made it to Spain and the Comintern was to regulate and organise this effort, with national Communist parties serving as recruiting agents and putting the infrastructure in place for volunteers to travel. This initiative would swiftly take hold of the popular imagination and led to more than 32,000 making the often-dangerous journey across seas and mountains to the blockaded Republic. The International Brigades soon became something much greater and more significant than Moscow likely ever imagined or intended and remain to this day the most unique, well known and indeed perhaps most written about aspect of the Spanish Civil War. International volunteers would fight in practically every major battle of the Civil War and were key shock troops in the Republican People's Army. They were, on the whole, committed, brave soldiers who fought against the odds in a losing struggle – one that became theirs not by nationality but by conviction. They lacked training and modern equipment. They were sometimes poorly led and often their actions proved futile. Contrary to the commonly held image, they were mostly working-class Communists and activists rather than middle-class poets and writers. But these facts make their story no less extraordinary, nor indeed less heroic. More than eighty years later their idealism and spirit of sacrifice represent an enduring example of heroism in an age when Europe was being consumed by darkness and war. It is the history of these valiant Brigades, their creation, recruitment, training, discipline and, most importantly, their combat record, that this present volume concerns. Much has been written about practically every aspect of the International Brigades, but the focus here is on military history and combat performance, an area that has, in the English language at least, played second fiddle to political, social and oral histories to date.

First, the formation, composition, organisation and training of Brigades, as well as the weapons and equipment they used, will be discussed at length in the first chapter. Then the book will follow the Brigades in combat throughout the civil war. The narrative begins with the volunteers' baptism of fire in the winter of 1936/7, when a series of battles in central Spain decided the fate of Madrid. With precious little training or

Men of the People's Army 46th 'Shock' Division being reviewed by senior Republican figures. (*Left to right*) Republican Prime Minister Juan Negrín, President Manuel Azaña, General José Miaja, Major Valentín González (*el campesino*), Major Enrique Líster.

equipment, the Brigades somehow held their own against Franco's finest troops, albeit at huge cost. During 1937 the People's Army went onto the offensive, and the Brigades were frequently the tip of the spear, bearing the brunt of some of the war's most brutal battles. After disaster in the spring of 1938, the Brigades were rebuilt (using mainly Spanish conscripts) in time for one final, bloody throw of the dice at the Battle of the Ebro. Readers familiar with Hemingway's *For Whom the Bell Tolls*, Orwell's *Homage to Catalonia* or even the 2006 civil war fantasy film *Pan's Labyrinth* must cast aside their preconceptions of the Spanish Civil War. It was not a guerrilla war, as portrayed by Hemingway and in Del Toro's film. Orwell, meanwhile, is probably the most famous foreign volunteer in the conflict and yet he was never a member of the International Brigades, instead joining the POUM, a small, anti-Stalinist party, and their amateurish militia. His description of several months on a quiet, inconsequential front could not be further removed from the epic struggles in which the Brigaders would find themselves time and again. It is their neglected story of idealism and incompetence to which we now turn.

Chapter 1

Antifascistas: The International Brigades

Formation and Recruitment

Following the Soviet decision to intervene in Spain in September 1936, the Comintern dispatched a number of officials, led by André Marty and Luigi Longo (known in Spain as Gallo) to organise the numerous foreign volunteers already arriving into an International Brigade. Months before, the Comintern had set aside 1,000 million francs to finance and arm a brigade of 5,000 volunteers. Eventually, more than 32,000 men from over fifty countries would serve in its ranks. Even before the creation of the Brigades, thousands had flocked to Spain to fight for the Republic. Many of the first to volunteer were athletes and activists in Barcelona at the outbreak of war for the People's Olympiad, a left-wing protest games set up in response to the official Olympics being held in Nazi Germany that year. Next, scores of artists, writers and intellectuals, individuals with the financial and cultural capital to make an international trip, found their way to Spain. They were joined by less well-to-do volunteers, mainly from

Mugshot of Luigi Longo ('Gallo'), arrested as part of Mussolini's crackdown on political opposition. Longo would go on to become the leader of the Italian communist party in the 1960s and 1970s.

neighbouring France, many of whom were exiles from Germany, Italy and other right-wing dictatorships, who now saw a chance to fight fascism. Even before the Comintern had begun to organise the Brigades, hundreds of spontaneous volunteers had arrived in Spain, most finding their way into the disorganised but spirited worker and peasant militias created by trade unions and political parties when the Republican government made the decision to arm the people just days into the conflict. However, with infrastructure put in place by Communist parties around the world, thousands more, mainly working-class, volunteers could make the trip, even if they did not have the money or documents required. Soon, there was a steady flow of Brigaders arriving from around Europe, via Paris, where large groups were mustered and then smuggled across the French frontier. The real credit for melding the disparate, chaotic elements that found their way to Spain into the International Brigades must go to the organising efforts of Longo. He arrived to find many different groups of volunteers languishing in various barracks and militia headquarters, frustrated at their lack of action. After being fobbed off by the Republican authorities, the Spanish Communist Party offered Longo one of their militia bases at Albacete, equidistant between Madrid and Valencia. Arriving on 12 October 1936 to find no accommodation, weapons, uniforms or equipment, in less than a month Longo and other Comintern officials would have not just created a training and administrative base for the Internationals, but also founded, equipped, armed and, by a liberal definition of the term, trained, two International Brigades numbering more than 3,500 men from at least a dozen countries. Not only that, but by 12 November both brigades were in combat in the desperate defence of Madrid, where they would unquestionably fight with great courage and determination, even if they were found wanting in terms of skill and tactics, winning a heroic reputation for themselves.

Base reports indicate that by the end of April 1938, 31,369 foreign volunteers had served in the Brigades, with the largest national groups being the French (8,778), Poles (3,034), Germans and Austrians (3,026), Italians (2,908) and Americans (2,274). There would be one final glut of arrivals in the spring and early summer of 1938 when the French government temporarily reopened the frontier and Communist parties around the globe stepped up their recruitment drives. Most scholars estimate a total of between 32,000 and 35,000 volunteers serving in the Brigades over the course of the war, although there is clearly no definitive figure and a margin of error of several thousand. Given the figure provided by the

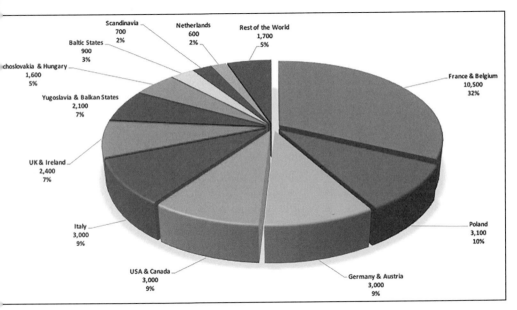

Figure 1. Volunteers by nationality.

Albacete base just five months before the International Brigades were withdrawn, the lower end of the estimate seems most likely. Figure 1 shows the
breakdown of the volunteers by nationality, aggregating figures from a
number of modern estimates and the final report quoted above to give a
rough total of 32,600 Brigaders.

There was a whole host of reasons why volunteers went to Spain,
although, as can be seen from Figure 2, many belonged to Communist or
other left-wing parties and were clearly ideologically motivated. It is
thought that between 60 and 75 per cent of the Brigaders were Communists, although the figure varied depending on nationality, with a higher
percentage of Americans being party members than, for example, French

Figure 2. Political affiliation of British and Irish volunteers (where given). Note: more than
500 volunteers also listed membership of a trade union. This figure has not been included
as there are likely to be many volunteers who were members of both party and trade union
and would therefore be counted twice. (*Baxell, 2007*)

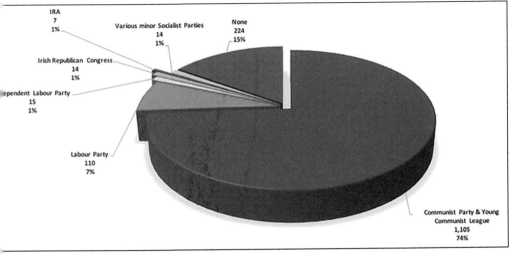

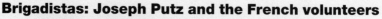

Brigadistas: Joseph Putz and the French volunteers

Despite making up the largest national group in the International Brigades, the combat performance of the French units in the civil war rank among the poorest. The same cannot be said of Joseph Putz, who was arguably one of the most talented men in the Internationals' ranks. Born in 1895, Putz had served with distinction as a junior officer in the First World War and, despite not being a Communist, had, on the strength of his military experience, been appointed commander of the Henri Barbusse battalion of the largely French 14th International Brigade upon its creation in December 1936. By February 1937 Putz was head of the Brigade and led it bravely in the bloody Jarama battle, being wounded and replaced with the rather less competent Jules Dumont. Dumont was also a decorated First World War veteran, and a prominent Communist, but his leadership of the 14th was to prove disastrous. At Segovia in May and June 1937 the French lost a thousand men for virtually no gains and Dumont argued bitterly with his divisional commander General Walter, who perceived him as vain and arrogant. Nevertheless, Dumont's political connections kept him in his post for over a year, and so once Putz had again recovered, he could not take up his old command. Instead, he was one of just a handful of foreigners who made it to the beleaguered Republican Northern Zone, where his military expertise was clearly valued and he commanded a division of the Basque army during the defence of Bilbao. Wounded several times, and eventually promoted to the rank of lieutenant colonel, one might speculate that had as fine a soldier as Putz had more than a few weeks in charge of the 14th Brigade, its record might not have been so lacklustre. After the civil war he moved to Algeria, but he was called up when the Second World War broke out. Fortunate to have been in the colonies during the Fall of France, Putz, now holding the rank of captain in the French army, put himself at the disposal of one of the leading figures in the emerging Free French military, General Leclerc. With this charismatic cavalry commander, Putz would fight in the North Africa campaign and, once their unit became the 2nd Free French armoured division, in the Battle of Normandy. Rising once again to the rank of lieutenant colonel, Putz for a time commanded the 3rd Battalion, Chad Infantry Regiment, a motorised infantry unit of French Foreign Legionnaires, whose 9th Company, known as *La Nueve*, was mostly composed of exiled Spanish Republican veterans. These men would be the first Allied troops to liberate Paris on 24 August 1944, riding half-tracks named 'Brunete' and 'Guadalajara', along with other civil war monikers. Putz himself would be killed in action, as always leading from the front, in the Battle of the Colmar Pocket in January 1945, aged just 49.

volunteers, likely due to the differing level of commitment required for a journey across the Atlantic compared to a hop over the Pyrenees. Less than half of the Italian recruits were Communists, with significant contingents of Anarchists and Republicans in the ranks of Italian International Brigade units, showing how the allegiances of volunteers reflected to some extent the political landscape of their home country. For activists on the left around the world, from the summer of 1936 for at least a year, the Spanish Revolution and Civil War became the most important international issue; 'Spain became your lifeblood' remembered one Glasgow volunteer of the time before he was able to enlist. In the 1930s, a polarised age of mass mobilisation, the issue of Spain seems to have had a great impact on the popular imagination, even more so than Hitler's seizure of power for instance. For many, both those who went to fight and those who supported the Spanish Republic in other ways, the stakes were huge; it was widely held that the advance of fascism could be checked in Spain, that Hitler and Mussolini's expansionist ambitions could be thwarted, that no less than a world war could be avoided, if the dictators were stopped on Spanish soil. Scores of veterans held on to this misconception for decades, many until their dying days. The vast majority of volunteers had little or no understanding of the complex political events which had led to the outbreak of the civil war, as described in this volume's

Introduction. In fairness, the world press of the time would not have provided much coverage of Spanish domestic issues. What Brigaders did hear about, however, was the military rebellion of 1936 which triggered the conflict, perceived by many news outlets as an attempt to crush democracy by force. Even more exciting to countless Left-wingers were the reports that soon followed of social revolution and of workers and peasants valiantly and spontaneously defending their Republic against reactionary generals. Perhaps they also read of the brutality and terror unleashed by Franco's armies as they advanced across Spain, murdering tens of thousands of potential opponents, most infamously in Badajoz. And the greatest spur to action of all were the widespread reports of Italian and German intervention, including stories of civilians bombed by Nazi aircraft. This was the first time air power was used against European cities on a large scale and naturally the reactions to the consequences were horror and consternation. For thousands of Leftists around the world, these stories were impossible to ignore. The rise of Hitler and Mussolini had come about without much of a fight, and both dictators were flexing their foreign policy muscles at the time, with the Western powers turning a blind eye, to the frustration of many in Britain, France, the United States and elsewhere. Here in Spain was a chance to actually fight fascism and defend democracy and revolution. The great debates of the age seemed to be being played out in combat on Spanish soil. Certainly, more than 10,000 volunteers came from nations living under authoritarianism, such as Germany, Italy, Austria, Poland, Yugoslavia and others. Some were living in political exile, while others slipped out of their home country, with stories of German Brigaders hanging on to the underside of trains crossing the French border. For both exiles and those leaving a right-wing regime to fight in Spain, there was little hope of returning home. And yet for Italians and Germans in particular, here was a chance to fight Hitler or Mussolini when they could not do so in their native countries.

While many volunteers, both before and during their time in Spain, had only a limited understanding of the political debates that racked the Republic, and generally accepted the Communist Party line they were sold by their commissars and commanders, what comes through in countless memoirs and accounts of veterans is the sense that they 'did the right thing' in going to Spain. They were defending democracy and fighting fascism, standing up to Hitler and his ilk even though their own governments did nothing. They were safeguarding the democracy and rights of the Spanish people. For those less aware of politics (and some volunteers were relatively apolitical) what they heard of Spain seemed to paint a clear picture of underdog and villain, with no doubt as to which side they should be supporting. This is why the International Brigades ended up attracting so many thousands of idealistic and passionate young men to fight in a foreign land. The American volunteer James Lardner, in a letter to his mother, articulated well the complex mixture of reasons that inspired Brigaders to risk life and limb, as well as to leave their lives and homelands behind:

> Because I believe that fascism is wrong and must be exterminated, and that liberal democracy or more probably Communism is right. Because my joining the I.B. might have an effect on the amendment of the neutrality act in the United States. Because after the war is over I shall be a more effective anti-fascist. Because in my ambitious quest for knowledge in all fields, I cannot afford in this age to overlook war … Because I am mentally lazy and should like to do some physical work for a change. Because I need something remarkable in my background to make up for my unfortunate self-consciousness in social relations.[1]

It is true that a small number of volunteers went somewhat unwillingly. By the latter stages of the war, as the flow of volunteers dried up in the face of the perilous military situation of the Republic, there is evidence that Communist parties leaned on eligible members to 'do the right thing'. On the other hand, some parties prevented their best cadres from going, judging that they were too valuable to lose. There is virtually no evidence for various myths that circulated suggesting recruits were tricked into going with promises of highly paid jobs or were somehow duped or unaware of the dangers they would face. Once the first International Brigade casualty figures from the winter battles of 1936/7 were reported, no volunteer could have been under the illusion that the war in Spain was a picnic. Neither were the Brigaders mercenaries in the traditional sense of the word; initially pay was just 3 pesetas a day, and the value of the Republican peseta outside Spain soon collapsed, rendering service in the Brigades rather futile as a money-making enterprise. Historian Cecil Eby actually writes that the first American volunteers were not expecting to be paid at all. Undoubtedly some volunteers were spurred simply by a sense of adventure, especially amidst the mass unemployment of the Great Depression and the lack of opportunities it created. However, the majority undertook the perilous journey to Spain, which was for many European volunteers a one-way trip owing to the nature of their homeland's regimes, due to political commitment to the Republic's cause, as evidenced by the proportion of Brigaders who were activists or members of left-wing parties and unions.

Unsurprisingly, given the majority were Communist or Socialist, an overwhelming proportion of the International Brigaders were working class. Perhaps as a result of the literature about the Spanish Civil War by the likes of Orwell, Lee and Hemingway, there is a popular misconception that the Brigades were made up of poets, writers and intellectuals. While it is true that a striking number of intellectuals and artists did visit or write for the Republic, upwards of 80 per cent of those who actually fought were from working-class stock. Using archival records, historian Richard Baxell has been able to identify the professions of the British and Irish recruits (*see* Figure 3). More than 80 per cent came from working-class employment – manufacturing, transport, various trades and mining. Mining and shipbuilding in particular were highly politicised occupations with a strong Communist and union presence and, as a result, high proportions of British volunteers came from the mines of South Wales and the shipyards of Tyneside, Glasgow and Sunderland. Docks such as Liverpool also provided large contingents and seaman was in fact the fourth most common profession listed. The volunteers came overwhelmingly from big cities, and naturally London and Dublin provided the lion's share of British and Irish volunteers: 520 from the former and more than 25 per cent of the Irish from the latter. A similar urban industrial

Figure 3. Professions of British and Irish volunteers (where given). (*Baxell, 2007*)

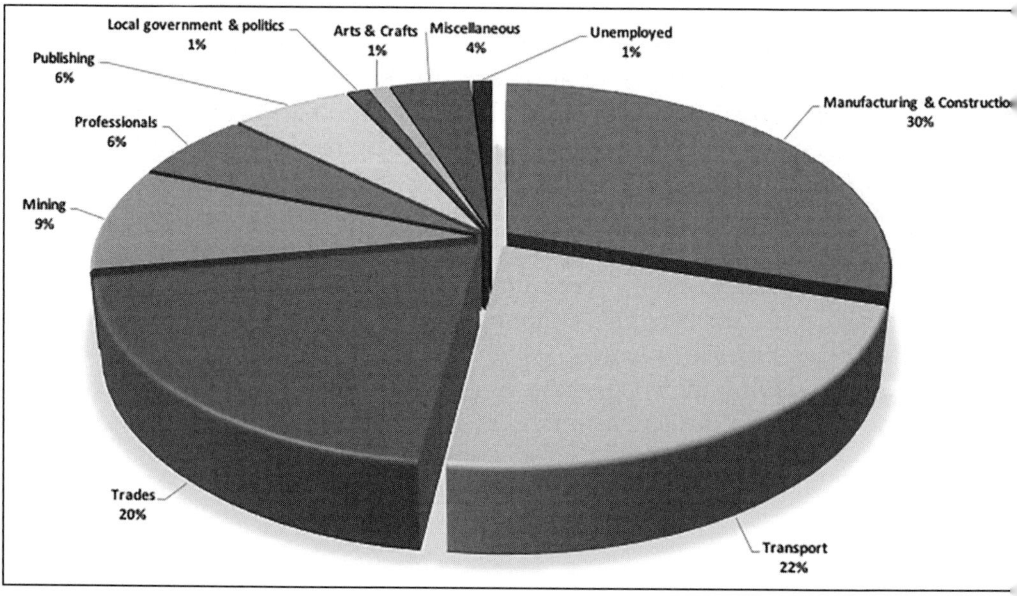

picture is found among the American recruits, with New York predominant and large numbers coming from the European immigrant and Jewish communities. Given that religion was not recorded on arrival, there are no accurate figures for the number of Jews but some estimates put Jewish volunteers at 7,000, meaning that for a fifth of the Brigaders the fight against fascism held particular significance. Just 1 per cent of volunteers listed themselves as unemployed, although likely the real figure was somewhat higher, with many men probably recording their trade or previous employment, even if they were out of work, especially given the shame attached to long-term unemployment at the time. Strikingly, Baxell also found that more than 25 per cent of volunteers who gave their date of birth were over the age of 30, refuting the idea that the volunteers were all young, naïve idealists. We must ignore the stereotypical image of the Brigader as an Orwell-type figure. Instead, the picture we develop of a typical International Brigader is a continental European Communist or Socialist of working-class background, a union member most likely employed in heavy industry and aged in their mid-to-late 20s.

While thousands of volunteers from across the globe made up the majority of the International Brigades, they were in fact not entirely international. Spaniards fought with the Brigaders from their very earliest actions, with Republican militiamen being integrated into General Kléber's defence of University City. He wrote to his superiors in Moscow that Spanish units actually wanted to join the International Brigades at this time, inspired by their heroic example. By the spring of 1937 most Brigades had one or more Spanish battalion to bolster their fighting strength, and at the same time Spanish companies were added to worn-out International battalions. At this stage the Spaniards were volunteers, keen to fight with the famous Internationals, but by 1938, when the flow of foreigners had all but dried up, and the Republic was scraping the bottom of the manpower barrel, scores of conscripts made up the numbers of the International Brigades, with only a small, hardened core of veterans – officers and NCOs mainly – in each unit actually being non-Spanish. By mid-1938, therefore, the Brigades were more foreign-led than true foreign units. Moreover, relations between Spaniards and Internationals were not always comradely. Comintern reports note that once brigades became majority Spanish, some resented having to serve under foreign officers. At other times Brigade volunteers showed disdain for their Spanish colleagues, considering them cowardly or not valuing them as much as the national group of a particular unit. For example, the Polish commander

General Walter complained that the predominantly German 11th Brigade never knew the casualties of their Spanish contingent, but always reported exact figures for the Internationals killed, wounded or missing. American Brigader Milton Wolff wrote that during the chaotic retreats of April 1938, the Lincoln-Washington battalion effectively abandoned their Spanish company in combat, hoping to escape encirclement as darkness fell. Nevertheless, this was not always the case; Walter noticed a significant increase in cooperation and respect between the Germans and Spaniards of the 11th Brigade during the Battle of Teruel, while Wolff would write poignantly of his grief at the death of a Spanish lieutenant serving under him at the Battle of the Ebro, whom he had designated as his successor.

Command, Organisation and Equipment

Initially, command of the International Brigades was entrusted entirely to Red Army or GRU (Soviet military intelligence) officers of non-Russian origin, with Generals Kléber, Lukács, Gomez, Walter and Gal taking initial command of the 11th–15th Brigades respectively. All these were *noms de guerre* for Manfred Stern, Máté Zalka, Wilhelm Zaisser, Karol Świerczewski and János Gálicz, all non-Russians. Zaisser was a German Communist who had gone to Moscow after Hitler came to power, while Świerczewski was a Pole who had lived in Imperial Russian territory before the Revolution. Kléber, Lukács and Gal, as well as other Brigade leadership figures such as Ćopić, had served in the Austro-Hungarian army in the First World War and had been captured on the Eastern Front. The prison camps of Tsarist Russia had proved a prime breeding-ground for Bolshevism and they had then joined the Reds once revolution, and subsequently civil war, broke out in 1917. Sent to Spain, these men used false names and their original or assumed nationalities to mask direct Soviet intervention; for instance, Kléber told reporters he was a naturalised Canadian citizen, while Zaisser operated under the pseudonym Goméz posing as a Mexican national! The administration and political leadership of the Brigades and the base at Albacete were overseen by Comintern functionaries of a variety of nationalities, with the French revolutionary André Marty as the deeply unpopular chief commissar and Gallo (the Italian Communist Luigi Longo) as the Brigade Inspector General. Meanwhile, command of individual battalions went to men from whatever nation predominated in that particular unit. In the first weeks of the Brigades some leaders were chosen simply for their linguistic skills,

The 'butcher of Albacete': the brutal French communist André Marty, chief commissar of the Brigades.

with battalions often containing a number of nationalities. In general, military experience, particularly in the First World War, was seen as vital, while Communist Party membership was certainly preferable for the Brigade's Comintern organisers. Table 1 below demonstrates the predominance of Communists who had fought in the last war. Tom Wintringham met both criteria and would lead the British battalion into their first battle; he would later be succeeded by figures such as Fred Copeman and Sam Wild, Communists too young to have served in the war but with some previous military service. Many of the Irish officers, such as Kit Conway and Frank Ryan, had fought in the IRA, although Paddy O'Daire had experience in the regular Irish army. Most continental European nations had strong Communist parties and a plethora of First World War experience to draw on, so there were plenty of candidates for battalion leadership. The most notable exception was Randolfo Pacciardi, a First World War hero but Republican rather than Communist in his politics, a fact that would eventually lead to clashes with the Brigade leadership and

Table 1. Leading Officers of the International Brigades. Red Army/Soviet Intelligence personnel in **bold**.

Leading Officer	Rank	Nationality	Highest post attained	Communist?	First World War experience?
'Walter' (Karol Świerczewski)	**General**	**Polish**	**Commanded 35th Division**	**Yes**	
'Emilio Kléber' (Manfred Stern)	**General**	**Romanian/Ukrainian (Austro-Hungarian Empire)**	**Commanded 45th Division**	**Yes**	**Yes**
'Pavol Lukács' (Máté Zalka)	**General**	**Hungarian**	**Commanded 45th Division**	**Yes**	**Yes**
'Gal' (János Gálicz)	**General**	**Hungarian**	**Commanded 15th Division**	**Yes**	**Yes**
'Goméz' (Wilhelm Zaisser)	**General**	**German**	**Albacete base commander**	**Yes**	**Yes**
'Hans' (Hans Kahle)	Lieutenant Colonel	German	Commanded 45th Division	Yes	Yes
Joseph Putz	Lieutenant Colonel	French	Commanded a Basque division		Yes
Randolfo Pacciardi	Lieutenant Colonel	Italian	Commanded 12th Brigade		Yes
'Jan Barwiński' (Józef Strzelczyk)	Lieutenant Colonel	Polish	Commanded 13th Brigade	Yes	
Jules Dumont	Lieutenant Colonel	French	Commanded 14th Brigade	Yes	Yes
Vladimir Čopić	Lieutenant Colonel	Yugoslavian	Commanded 15th Brigade	Yes	Yes
'Richard' or 'Hoffmann' (Richard Staimer)	Major	German	Commanded 11th Brigade	Yes	
'Otto Flatter' (Ferenc Münnich)	Major	Hungarian	Commanded 11th Brigade	Yes	Yes
Carlo Penchienati	Major	Italian	Commanded 12th Brigade	Yes	
'Karchenko' (Mikhail Khvatov)	**Major**	**Ukrainian**	**Commanded 13th Brigade**	**Yes**	**Not known**
Robert Merriman	Major	American	Acting commander of 15th Brigade		
Frank Ryan	Major	Irish	Adjutant to General Miaja		
George Nathan	Major	British	15th Brigade Chief of Staff		Yes

Note: The Italian Communist Nino Nanetti commanded the 12th Division at Guadalajara and a Basque division on the Northern Front but he does not seem to have commanded International troops before being killed in action in July 1937.

his departure. The situation was slightly different for the Americans, lacking First World War veterans. The Abraham Lincoln battalion's first leader was Bob Merriman, an economist of working-class stock but no party affiliation and nothing more than a few summers in his university's officer training corps to qualify him for the role. The Americans were subsequently led by a variety of Brigaders, both Communists such as Hans Amlie and Oliver Law, and non-Communists such as Phil Detro, but none had ever fought a war before Spain. Over time, outstanding volunteers would rise from battalion to brigade command, such as the German Hans Kahle, the aforementioned Pacciardi or the Pole Józef Strzelczyk, as the Soviet military appointees who had served as the original brigade commanders were promoted to lead divisions. The Brigades were certainly not always in capable hands, however; Jules Dumont would command first the Commune de Paris battalion, and then the French-Belgian 14th Brigade for over a year despite his incompetence and disagreements with his superiors, the retention of his command owing to his high standing in the Communist Party. Kahle and the Frenchman Joseph Putz were the only volunteers to reach divisional command, suggesting they were seen as special talents. Both had been officers in the First World War. By the spring of 1938, when the Red Army and GRU personnel were largely withdrawn, Spaniards would take over the leadership of many of the International Brigades and divisions, with these units by then in fact being majority Spanish, having been formally integrated into the Republican People's Army in October 1937. Throughout their existence, however, no International commanders produced any tactical innovations. The Soviet officers in high command positions were a decidedly mixed bag. Gal was sacked for incompetence only a few months after arriving in Spain, while Kléber's star faded soon after his famous defence of Madrid. On the other hand, experienced soldiers like Kléber and Walter certainly did a better job than amateur militia commanders in other People's Army units, for instance in halting the rout at the Battle of Brunete, and they were probably at the level of the better First World War commanders, albeit with twenty years of hindsight on their side. The Brigades were blessed with a number of officers, particularly at battalion level and below, who were brave leaders of men, who led by example and kept a cool head under fire. But these officers could rarely offer anything tactically other than inspiring their troops to take or hold an objective 'at all costs'. The best a Brigader could hope for in a commander was an officer who was primarily a military rather than a political appointee and one who had served in the

Commander: General Walter (Karol Świerczewski)

General Walter, the Pole Karol Świerczewski, was to command International Brigade troops in Spain continuously for nearly 18 months, longer than any other Red Army officer serving in the conflict. Świerczewski was born in 1897 in Warsaw, Poland, when in fact no state of Poland existed – rather it was ruled over by the Russian Tsar. From a poor family, he was working in a factory by the age of 12 and was evacuated to Moscow in 1915 in the face of the German advance in the First World War. There, the young Świerczewski found himself at the epicentre of revolution a few years later and he joined the Bolsheviks, fighting in the Russian Civil War and the Polish–Soviet War, being wounded in the latter. A long career in the Red Army followed until he was dispatched to Spain in late 1936. Under his *nom de guerre* Walter, he immediately took command of the 14th International Brigade, but its early experiences at Lopera in December 1936 were rather disastrous. Nevertheless, Walter was promoted to divisional command during the Jarama battle the following February and was regarded by the Spanish general Modesto as an expert in offensive operations. Perhaps this explains his frustration with the 14th Brigade's Jules Dumont during the failed Segovia offensive in April 1937. Such was the acrimony of their falling-out that the 14th was removed from Walter's division. Walter led the largely international 35th Division through the subsequent battles of Brunete, Belchite, Teruel and the Great Retreats, where they generally fought well. He also stands out in the historical record because of the frank honesty of his reports back to Moscow; he was by no means afraid to criticise the Brigades, their commanders or the Soviet advisers for the mistakes they made, although he also indulged in the Communist paranoia over the Fifth Column and Trotskyism. He was well regarded by the volunteers, as evidenced by one British veteran's memory of seeing the Pole during the Aragon disaster of 1938:

> He looked very tired. His uniform was torn in a number of places ... What a contrast was this visit by our Divisional General to his previous one at Mondéjar near Madrid. Then he looked so smart with his immaculately-cut uniform. We all felt very sorry for him now as he was a very popular officer. He alone amongst us knew how bad things were.
>
> (Clark, 1984, p. 78.)

After the civil war Walter returned to the Soviet Union and continued to serve in the Red Army in the Second World War, but he suffered from alcoholism and was deliberately deprived of important commands. In the final phase of the war, as the Soviets advanced across Poland and into Germany, he took command of the Polish Second Army, a Polish-recruited unit within the Red Army, and was blamed for their excessive casualties in the some of the war's last battles. In 1946 Świerczewski was appointed as Deputy Defence Minister in the new Communist regime in Poland but was killed the following year while directing an operation against Ukrainian insurgents.

First World War. Unfortunately, not all were so fortunate and heavy casualties could often be attributed to unimaginative frontal attacks.

Attached to each unit from company size upwards was a commissar. Brigades and divisions also had a commissariat made up of several staff responsible for propaganda and political education. The role of the commissar was a varied one, and somewhat different from that in the Russian Civil War. In the Red Army the commissar had originally been a party representative who ensured that the former Tsarist officers who held many of the command positions remained loyal to the Bolshevik regime. In Spain the question of loyalty was not a major issue – as we have already seen, the Brigaders on the whole were highly political and unlikely to

A roll call at the International Brigade base in Albacete. (*IWM*)

want to go over to the Francoists. Instead, the role of the commissar was to maintain morale and discipline, to ensure the welfare of the troops and to educate the men on political matters. In the opinion of one veteran, the importance of the commissars in the International Brigades has been exaggerated:

I think probably the commissars in the International Brigade were not so important as they may have been in the Spanish units, because we had among the men of the International Brigade an extremely high proportion of people who under other circumstances would themselves have been what you may call commissar material. That's to say, they were shop stewards and trade union officials and Labour Party officials and people of this sort who ... naturally had a political leadership role, in their own communities, in their own factories and so on. So we had lots of people who were commissars without holding the rank of commissar.[2]

On the other hand, the role of the commissar developed during the war from a mere political cheerleader, with many effectively serving as the right-hand man of the unit commander, carrying messages, motivating the troops and leading charges. Furthermore, as more and more Spanish conscripts filled the ranks of the International units, commissars had to adopt the role seen more frequently in regular People's Army units – namely educating the men as to the reasons why the war was being fought and trying to inspire zeal in reluctant troops. Before the Battle of the Ebro, after receiving a batch of conscripts from Alicante, the commissars of the Abraham Lincoln battalion, many of whom could speak little Spanish, had the responsibility of instructing the young recruits in the causes of their own country's civil war and the dangers of fascism. Additionally, the role of the commissar was to look after the interests of the men and take complaints to the correct authority. One American volunteer described succinctly, if perhaps overly positively, the commissar's task and the relations between the ranks in the International Brigades:

> a commissar, was responsible to us. Meetings were called at his, or our, request, where every problem of discipline, of food, clothing, shelter, military orders, mail, tobacco (or largely the absence thereof) and personal behavior was thrashed out. The majority opinion ruled; it was the commissar's obligation to see that abuses and complaints were referred to the proper authority, and to implement the will of the soldiers as well as the desires of the command. It was his obligation to explain (and ours to understand) the conduct of the war ... He was entrusted with the political education of soldiers, which was at a high level among the Internationals ... These soldiers not only knew how to obey, but they understood the reasons for their obedience, and the rigid discipline that was imposed on them in action was self-imposed within reasonable limits ... their complaints and their suggestions were solicited and desired by the command. Out of hours they addressed their officers as 'comrade', or by their first names. They were so addressed by their officers; and this solidarity within our army accounted for military miracles.[3]

The People's Army Commissariat motto was 'First to advance, last to retreat' and many commissars were well liked stalwarts of International units who had good relations with the men. They were usually individuals with experience in working-class organisations and unions and therefore understood the soldiers under their command. What is noticeable from the accounts of veterans is how keenly felt was the loss of a good commissar and also how much morale was negatively affected by a bad commissar –

Italian anarchists of the Malatesta Column photographed in Barcelona. More than 300 Italian anarchists joined the International Brigades. Although women did fight in the Republican militias seen in the war's first months, they were not permitted combat roles in the People's Army or International Brigades.

The Commissariat had a number of tools at its disposal, including printing presses for the production of trench newspapers, and, rather more unusually, sound trucks, one of which was used to great effect at the battle of Belchite to encourage Nationalist surrender. *(Tamiment Library and Robert F. Wagner Labor Archive)*

for example, many in the Canadian-American Mackenzie-Papineau battalion resented their first commissar, Joe Dallet, for his disciplinarian nature and strict adherence to Communist doctrine. On the eve of their first battle, there was a meeting demanding his removal, although Dallet retained his post. In an attempt to regain some popularity and prove he practised what he preached, Dallet led the battalion's charge, being quickly cut down:

> He was hit in the groin and suffered agonies, yet he waved back the First-Aid men, refusing to let them risk sure death in an attempt to reach him. He was trying to crawl back unaided when a fresh burst from a machine gun blasted life out of him. Joe knew he had to die to redeem the prestige of a commissar, to justify in his own eyes the path he had followed in Spain – a victim of his own Communist training.[4]

At first, the organisation of the International units resembled somewhat the revolutionary worker and peasant militias created by Leftist unions and parties at the outbreak of civil war. Squad and company leaders were elected by vote and orders were discussed and debated by the men together. A small group of British volunteers actually voted on which battalion they wanted to join! Soon, however, a more formal organisation and hierarchy had to be introduced, despite the fervour many volunteers felt for the idea of a 'democratic army'. Indeed, there was not a little resentment when, in October 1937, the Brigades were formally integrated into the People's Army and parade drill, saluting and other such symbols of military hierarchy and discipline were introduced. In total, seven different International Brigades were created during the war, although the 11th to the 15th were the longest-lived. Within each Brigade there was a mixture of national groups, formed into battalions that were often named after a national or left-wing hero from that country, or else a significant event. Many of the Brigades actually came to be known by the moniker of the most famous battalion within it; for example, the 12th International Brigade was widely referred to as the Garibaldis, named after the famous Italian Garibaldi battalion within it (for more details *see* Appendix). Each International Brigade consisted of several infantry battalions, usually three or four but occasionally more. By the summer of 1937 most Brigades had an all-Spanish battalion, while the rest were International, divided up along national or linguistic lines. Each battalion, commanded by a captain, would contain three rifle and one machine-gun company. Again, from roughly mid-1937, one rifle company was usually all-Spanish. The captain would have a small staff comprising an adjutant, commissar, interpreter, armourer, medical officers, chronicler and a team of runners. The machine-gun company was equipped with eight machine guns, most often Maxims, crewed by up to five men each. The rifle companies were roughly 100 men strong and divided into three platoons, denoted by the Spanish term *pelotón* (or in German-speaking units *zug*), each with around thirty men. The platoon was split into eight-man sections. Each company was commanded by a lieutenant and a commissar, with a sergeant leading a *pelotón* and a corporal or *Cabo* in charge of a section. At most, battalions numbered 600–700 men, but they were usually understrength.

At first the Brigade commander would have been a Red Army/GRU general but later they were lieutenant colonels or, more commonly, majors drawn from the volunteers. In addition to the infantry battalions, the Brigade commander had at his disposal an anti-tank battery of three guns, a cavalry squadron, and a Brigade commissariat with sound-truck and printing presses, as well as his own headquarters staff and services. These staff included an adjutant, a secretary, a chief of staff, a chief of operations,

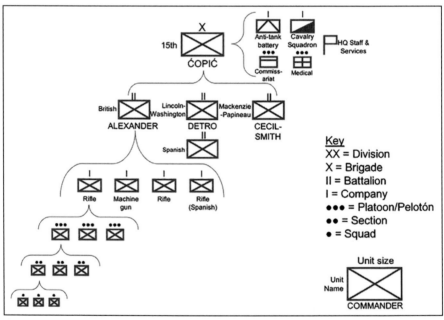

Figure 4. Theoretical establishment of an International Brigade (based on the 15th International Brigade, winter 1937/8).

Republican forces were short of quality artillery and in particular shells. The International Brigades often did not have their own artillery and had to rely on paltry support from divisional or corps batteries.

a chief of services, a topographical department and a chief of information in charge of keeping records. Brigade services included a sanitary section, a supply/quartermaster department, field kitchens, auto-park, post office and a transmissions and communications department. The organisation of the International Brigades mirrored the so-called mixed brigades that were the basic building blocks of the People's Army. While it might appear, and indeed it was intended, that each Brigade was so equipped that it was effectively an independent, self-reliant fighting unit, in reality the structure of the mixed brigade was unwieldy, overly bureaucratic and wasted too much manpower in staff roles. It must be noted also that the International Brigades were rarely, if ever, at full strength and so the organisation laid out above was an ideal standard that was not always attained.

There was never a single formal uniform in the International Brigades; in fact, the only uniform aspect of the appearance of volunteers was their variety. Initially, during the Madrid battles of late 1936 and early 1937, most Brigaders wore a hodgepodge of vaguely military-style attire that reflected whatever the Republic and Comintern had to hand. A brown corduroy uniform known as a *mono* was common, as were British leather trench jerkins. Throughout the war woollen ponchos were used in cold weather, as were long great coats, civilian or military. By mid-1937 there was more uniformity, although a standard uniform as such was never

Internationals of the 11th or 12th Brigade fighting in the University City sector, November 1936. This photograph illustrates the typical uniform of the early Brigaders.
(© *Robert Capa* © *International Center of Photography/Magnum Photos*)

achieved. In general, soldiers wore tan or khaki battledress (acquired from numerous sources), not dissimilar to the Second World War uniform of the British army. Sam Browne belts were common, and some officers favoured a black leather windcheater jacket, known as a *cazadora*. Webbing was usually the Spanish army's leather M1926 issue. Officers and NCOs would wear some insignia of rank, either on their cap, beret, left chest or cuff, or indeed on a combination of the above. A sergeant's insignia was a red star above a single red vertical bar. Officers had a red star with horizontal gold bars, two for a lieutenant, three for a captain. More elaborate insignia distinguished higher ranks. Commissars' rank badges mirrored those of officers except that the red star was set in a red circular outline and the bars were also red. Some officers acquired more formal pre-civil war Spanish army or Republican People's Army dress uniforms, complete with shirt and tie, while others favoured civilian jumpers and jackets. Some soldiers wore a red star or, rarely, the three-pointed star of the International Brigades but in general most volunteers did not wear any sort of distinguishing badge or insignia. Headgear was even more varied.

Various caps and berets in olive, tan, navy or khaki were common. Highly popular was the *pasamontaña*, a soft woollen peaked cap which can be seen in many photographs of Brigaders in all seasons. Officers usually opted for either a beret with rank insignia, dress cap or less formal, baggy, unstiffened cap, or else a Spanish side-cap known as an *isabellino*. Steel

Volunteers wearing more standardised uniform and the popular Adrian helmet, early 1937, Jarama front. (*Tamiment Library and Robert F. Wagner Labor Archive*)

helmets were initially not issued to Brigaders; although they became more common from early 1937 onwards, they were certainly never ubiquitous. The most widely issued was the French Adrian helmet seen in both world wars, but some Brigaders used the Spanish M1926 type, somewhat resembling an enlarged German *Stalhelm*, or the rounded Czech M1930 type. Most veterans made a point of recording in their memoirs the moment they were issued with their unusual footwear, which for many was actually as they set off to climb the Pyrenees and illegally cross the French border into Spain. The volunteers were provided with rope-soled canvas espadrilles called *alpargatas* which were generally disliked and unsuitable for poor weather or rough terrain. Various other boots and shoes were naturally found to replace them when they wore out.

Upon deployment, during the Republic's existential crisis of November 1936–February 1937, the International Brigades were issued with a real mixture of generally poor weaponry. At this time the Republicans were critically short of arms of all kinds. Franco's Rebels had gained control of the majority of the Spanish army's firearms and ordnance at the outbreak

Officers of the 15th International Brigade exhibiting a variety of uniforms. Captain Hugh Slater (*left*), Chief of Operations, wears the full People's Army staff captain uniform. Lieutenant Colonel Vladimir Ćopić (*centre*), Brigade commander, has a pre-civil war Spanish uniform with People's Army cap, while Captain Sam Wild (*right*), British battalion commander, displays a more casual approach with leather jacket and beret complete with captain's insignia. (*RGASPI*)

of war, and this advantage had only grown over the first months of the conflict as they advanced rapidly. Furthermore, the Non-Intervention Agreement established by the major powers banned the sale to both factions of any and all supplies that could be used to conduct the war. While Italy, Germany and the Soviet Union flaunted this agreement, it was a serious disadvantage to the Republic as it meant that the government could not purchase arms legally on the open market from manufacturers or arms dealers. Instead, they had to rely on shipments from, on the one hand, Russia, over 3000 kilometres distant and subject to interception by Axis naval forces, and on the other hand, the black market. Both the Soviets and dodgy black-market dealers ripped off the desperate Republicans and sold substandard, obsolete and unwanted equipment. The Polish army deliberately off-loaded their militarily useless stocks on the Republic at exorbitant prices, a mixture of German, French, Austrian

An African-American volunteer of the Mackenzie-Papineau battalion firing his Mosin-Nagant. He is wearing the *pasamontaña*. (*Tamiment Library and Robert F. Wagner Labor Archive*)

and Russian First World War arms that had been in storage for decades. The Soviets cynically used their new ally as a dumping ground for surplus materiel from the Russian Civil War, the First World War and even the Russo-Japanese War of 1904–5. Some Brigaders tell of seeing hallmarks from the 1890s or earlier on their rifles, which were so worn that the muzzles were smooth. All this meant that the Republic ended up using dozens of weapons from all around the world, all chambered to different calibres of ammunition, some lacking sights, cleaning kits or instructions; it was nothing short of a logistical nightmare. Such were the shortages that in some cases olive oil was used to clean the rifles, ineffectively it must be said. Meanwhile, the Germans and Italians met Franco's arms demands in a far more standardised manner and allowed him to pay on credit or in kind with mineral resources. In their first battles the International Brigades employed a wide variety of weapons, using whatever the Republic had been able to get its hands on at a time when Soviet aid was only just beginning to arrive. The first two International Brigades sent to the Battle for Madrid in November 1936 were issued with the St Étienne Mle 1907 machine gun, an awkward, bulky, unreliable French weapon. Reportedly, one French volunteer, recognising the weapon from his service in the First World War, simply burst out laughing. An even worse gun was the French Chauchat machine rifle (a type today termed a light machine gun), which frequently jammed despite having an extremely low rate of fire. While the American Colt M1895 machine gun that was also issued was somewhat better, the models in Spain often came with the wrong ammunition belts and these weapons too jammed in the hands of unfamiliar operators. Meanwhile, it appears that those unlucky first Brigaders were given a huge variety of old rifles. Tom Wintringham worked at the International Brigade base at Albacete during those first weeks:

> I have already described the rifles of the 12th [La Marseillaise] Battalion when it moved off to action five weeks before – derelict Swiss and Austrian things, Steyrs most of them, that never looked as if they would fire at all and did in the majority of cases jam quite seriously after the first bullet was fired through them. I remembered the odds and ends of rifles that some battalions of the foreign volunteers had 'made do' with for a time, until better stuff came through; clumsy bolts and sights battered to inaccuracy, a mixture of calibres and cartridges, Ross, Remington, Lebel, Japanese, Turkish, Polish rifles, Mexican Mausers, even cavalry carbines, all in odd lots.[5]

The Brigades were given no heavy weapons and were advised to combat tanks with petrol bombs. Indeed, throughout the Internationals' time in Spain, they found themselves outgunned owing to a lack of heavy ordnance. To the surprise of one US military observer, the Brigades were never issued with mortars, despite the simplicity and practicality of the weapon. Some Brigaders served in artillery units, but these were not directly attached to the International Brigades; indeed, one British volunteer serving in an artillery unit on the central front ended up serving for some months after the withdrawal and disbanding of the Brigades as the Republican authorities appeared to have forgotten about his little group. The only heavy weapons the International Brigades had at their disposal was a battery of anti-tank guns. In the spring and summer of 1937 each Brigade received three fine 45mm Soviet AT guns. As the Nationalist army had few tanks, and due to the lack of alternatives, more often than not these guns were deployed in infantry support roles. They proved adept in both the bunker-buster role, pummelling hardpoints of resistance into submission, and in breaking up waves of attacking enemy infantry.

A FIAT-Revelli Model 1914 machine gun, likely captured from Mussolini's troops in Spain, being used by Loyalist militiamen. This image highlights the unhelpful variety of weapons used by the Republic. (*Shutterstock, Everett Historical 238056874*)

Weapons: Rifles of the International Brigades

When the war broke out in 1936 the ordnance situation on the Republican side was desperate. Franco's forces were in control of most of the military's equipment and the Republic had to rely on rifles imported from abroad. The result was a hotchpotch of various guns in various calibres, many of them obsolescent. Among the mainstay weapons of the International Brigades were surplus Mosin Nagant rifles made in Russia. These guns were nicknamed 'Mexicanskis'; thousands had been sold to Mexico after the First World War before being sold to Spain. The Mosin Nagant was not made to the same standard as the Mauser rifles used by the Nationalists, and had a mixed reputation with the Brigaders who used it, but it was an acceptable enough rifle. Later in the war the Republican forces received shipments of a much better rifle – the Vz.24, a Czech-made version of the Mauser with an excellent reputation for accuracy and reliability. These guns arrived in time to be used at the Ebro in 1938. A volunteer described the moment the Lincoln-Washington battalion was issued with Czech Mausers in 1938:

> The shipment of rifles that they had been waiting for arrived. Beautiful new Czech Mausers. They looked much more formidable than the ancient Remingtons that had been standard issue … Holding the Mauser in his

Czech vz. 24 Mauser. (*Tamiment Library and Robert F. Wagner Labor Archive*)

Mosin-Nagants, often referred to as Mexicanskis.
(Tamiment Library and Robert F. Wagner Labor Archive)

hands, he forgot about the tanks, planes, artillery against which the Mausers would be little better than the old Remingtons. The heft of the rifle in his hands was reassuring. (Wolff, 2001, p. 273.)

Other rifles employed by the International Brigades included Austrian Mannlicher and Canadian Ross rifles, which both employed straight-pull bolts, and also the Enfield Pattern 13 rifle, which was supplied in very large quantities, with over 20,000 units being shipped to Spain. All were generally good rifles, but the mismatch of ammunition used for each type caused supply problems which remained a consistent obstacle in arming the Brigades.

The anti-tank batteries, at least in the 15th Brigade, came to be seen as something of an elite, hauling their guns into position in the middle of firefights and engaging at daringly close ranges.

By mid-1937 the Brigades had been issued better small arms from Soviet shipments to Spain. Throughout the war most volunteers were armed with one or another version of the Russian Mosin Nagant rifle, often referred to as a *Mexicanski*. These were both Russian and American-made (manufactured by Remington during the First World War), new 1931 models and older nineteenth-century examples. Their unusual nickname referred to the fact that Mexico had sent a shipment of Mosins to Spain, the rifles having been manufactured in the USA during the First World War to meet orders from Imperial Russia that went unfulfilled after the Revolution, resulting in the guns being sold to Mexico. Although these Mexican models represented only 5,000 of the hundreds of thousands of Mosin Nagants sold to Spain, the nickname stuck. Typical of Russian design, the Mosin Nagant was a sturdy rifle, perhaps a little inaccurate but tough, hard-wearing and relatively light. Many volunteers disliked the spike bayonet, which did not come with a scabbard as it was supposed to be mounted at all times. These ended up being used as tools or cooking utensils, and invariably were lost. In 1938 a number of International Brigade units actually had their Mosins replaced with brand-new Czech Mausers, exceptional rifles supplied by the sympathetic government of Czechoslovakia. The Maxim M1910 heavy machine gun was also very common and highly effective, although it was difficult to transport on its cumbersome wheeled chassis, which dug into the kidneys of those unlucky enough to have to haul them around on their back. Also widely used was the Maxim-Tokarev, a lighter variant of the M1910 that replaced the chassis with a bipod and omitted the water jacket. With the addition of a stock, the Maxim-Tokarev was much easier to set up and fire quickly. Other fine light machine guns with which the volunteers were equipped included the Soviet DP-28, a Polish copy of the American BAR and the Czech ZB-26, which was itself copied by the British in developing their famous Bren gun. Submachine guns were not used by the International Brigades and indeed were rather rare in the civil war. It must be said that, even though Brigader memoirs are full of complaints about the quality of their weapons, from mid-1937 onwards their small arms were in most cases equal to, if not superior to, those used by their Nationalist opponents. Indeed, the Francoists actually equipped their elite Moroccan troops with captured Czech Mausers. However, the Rebels' undoubted superiority

The fine M1937 45mm anti-tank (AT) gun supplied to the Republic by the Soviets. It was easily capable of knocking out any tank used by the Rebels.
(*Tamiment Library and Robert F. Wagner Labor Archive*)

in artillery and air power probably contributed significantly to the Brigaders' sense of being outgunned and made much more of a difference in large-scale battles. Lack of heavy firepower would lead to the Internationalists being forced to launch unsupported attacks on strong defensive positions time and again. For the most comprehensive guide to the firearms used in the civil war by both sides, *see* Freddy Clifford's appendix in *The People's Army in the Spanish Civil War: A Military History of the Republic and International Brigades*.

Discipline and Training

The International Brigades were a strict military to serve in, and Andre Marty at the head of the organisation was described by some as the 'Butcher of Albacete'. Several hundred (Marty admitted 500) international volunteers were executed during the war, although contrary to some accounts, these deaths were not the result of political purges or witch hunts for Trotskyists. Rather, the men who were killed were serial deserters, those found guilty of cowardice or passing information to the enemy, or those who had perpetrated serious crimes against civilians, such as rape. Far more common a punishment was a spell in a work camp, labour company or prison and several thousand Brigaders would be incarcerated, the vast majority from mid-1937 onwards as morale wavered badly.

Weapons: Machine guns of the International Brigades

The supply of machine guns for the Republicans quickly dried up shortly after the war began, with the capture of an important military arsenal at Oviedo by Franco's forces in early 1937. Thus, as with rifles, the Republic had to import foreign-made guns at an often extortionate cost. In service with the Spanish army before the war were French Hotchkiss and St Etienne machine guns, and International Brigaders found out the hard way that these guns were not particularly reliable or efficient, especially since many volunteers had no experience with them. The St Etienne model was so unpopular that it was soon replaced by the more reliable Lewis gun, which was more familiar to British users due to its extensive use during the First World War. The situation was also helped by the supply of some 3,000 old Maxim guns donated by the Soviets, which, despite their age, were a marked improvement over the Hotchkiss. One volunteer described the effectiveness of the Maxim against charging Moroccan *Regulares*:

> All guns would take part, working from left to right, sweeping the line together, until ordered to stop ... The order to fire ... was deadened by the blast of these concentrated heavy Maxims. The result was like mowing down wheat. As the bullets struck home, a still, thick black line appeared on the ground ... No cover was possible ... we were far above them, and the slaughter was almost complete. The firing continued until no hand moved in an attack which must have started with some 300 or 400 men. (Copeman, 1948, p. 93.)

The Soviets also supplied the more modern Maxim-Tokarev light machine guns, which had a very good reputation among the Republican ranks. It was supplied in bulk, with over 2,000 being delivered. The war in Spain was probably the most use these Tokarev guns saw, as they came too late for the First World War and too early for the Second World War.

Maxim-Tokarev. A lighter, air-cooled version of the Maxim, this was a fine weapon.
(*Tamiment Library and Robert F. Wagner Labor Archive*)

Maxim M1910, supplied by Russia to the Republic in great numbers. Superior to the Nationalist Hotchkiss, not least due to its rate of fire, at 600 rounds per minute, being around 200 rounds per minute higher than that of the M1914.

Hotchkiss M1914, the standard machine gun of the Spanish Army and used by both sides, especially the Nationalists. It was fed with awkward strip clips rather than a belt.

Confidential Soviet reports are candid about the desertion problem that plagued the Internationals at this time. In early August 1937 Albacete was so flooded with 'demoralized elements' that the base commander General Goméz felt it necessary to establish a concentration camp through which 4,000 men passed over a number of months. Some 80 per cent were returned to the front as 'good antifascist soldiers' after weeks of 'intensive political and military work'. The fate of the remaining 20 per cent, some 800 men, is not mentioned in the reports, leading Radosh *et al.* to speculate that these 'unreliables' were executed. This would leave a figure not so distant from Marty's own admission, although it seems hard to believe that every volunteer deemed unfit to return to the front was simply put up against a wall, especially as another Soviet report reveals that in a fifteen-week period in mid-1937 some 4,652 volunteers were repatriated, only 1,500 of them wounded. Given that this was at exactly the same time as Goméz's camp was sifting the wheat from the chaff, it would be a fair assumption to say many deemed unfit for further action were sent home, while it is clear that others were handed desk roles or non-combat postings. When battlefield executions of deserters (which are testified to in various Brigader accounts at desperate times) are factored in, the total number of Internationals shot was probably somewhere below 1,000, while between 4,000 and 6,000 were likely incarcerated. These figures are high for a force totalling no more than 35,000, although it must be remembered that the Brigades were repeatedly thrown into the toughest fights without adequate training or equipment and therefore demoralization and desertion were common. Additionally, these men were far from home and not fighting for their country; many believed, as volunteers, that they should have the right to leave when they wished. A system of home leave was simply not possible, although during the precious few rest periods afforded to the International Brigaders, a few days' leave in Madrid or Barcelona was common enough. Even scholars critical of the Brigades such as Richardson concede that the issue of home leave was an impossible one for the leadership to solve; with the Republic under blockade and service in the International Brigades illegal in many nations, including Britain and the USA, there could be no guarantee the volunteers would make it back, even if they wanted to. In an ordinary, national military, soldiers can be sent back on leave to their home country and if they go AWOL, the authorities can track them down. No such arrangements could be made for the International Brigades, which were viewed with suspicion by almost every capitalist government. Fighting a superior foe, repeatedly suffering heavy losses and military defeats, unable to return home to loved ones for even a few days, it is little wonder desertion, and subsequently punishment, was so common. Being an International Brigader was not, on the whole, a positive experience and many men looked for a way out. That serial deserters and other military criminals were shot should not, however, be seen as evidence of Stalinist terror, as some historians seem to suggest. In the context of European militaries of the twentieth century, the shooting of deserters and 'cowards' was common practice, even in 'democratic' armies such as those of Britain and France in the First World War. The International Brigades were harsh. But if they had not been, thousands more would presumably have taken a chance to go home once they realised the impossibility of the struggle or the sheer danger Brigaders were exposed to (remember that up to 93 per cent of volunteers were killed, wounded, captured or missing). In this context, while by no means moral, the severe disciplinary regime was at least rational; the men could not be allowed to believe that desertion was an easy option.

The International Brigade files in the Moscow archives are full of derogatory statements about the volunteers, with many described as politically weak or Trotskyist. This has led to some historians seeing the Brigades as part of Stalin's purges, where political non-conformists were imprisoned or killed. However, there is very little evidence that volunteers were executed for their politics – in all the secret Soviet reports and Comintern correspondence compiled in Radosh *et al.*'s *Spain Betrayed* there is no mention whatsoever of volunteers being shot, or even imprisoned, for their politics. The Soviet NKVD carried out brutal repression of Spanish Leftists, most notably the POUM, who openly criticised Stalin and the USSR, but there is no evidence their campaign of torture and murder extended to the International Brigaders. Far more likely, if a volunteer repeatedly disputed the party line, displayed 'defeatism' or argued with their officers or commissars, they would end up demoted or spending time in a labour company. It is hard to think of any military where the men can openly disrespect or challenge officers without reprimand, so while the political element does set the International Brigades apart somewhat, the disciplinary regime does not. The only difference in Spain was that malcontents might be disagreeing about the nature of revolution rather than food, shelter, tactics or the numerous other complaints rankers commonly express. Of more than 2,000 British and Irish volunteers, there is definite evidence for the executions of only two men, one for attempting

REPÚBLICA ESPAÑOLA

45 DIVISIÓN
XIII Brigada Internacional
"DOMBROWSKI"

ESTADO MAYOR

Núm. *138*

SALVOCONDUCTO

expedido a favor del *Capitán Chispa y teniente* ~~~~ *orber de Artillería*

de esta Brigada, para trasladarse de *Frente Huesca* a *Sariñena y regreso* siendo el objeto del viaje *Servicio de la Brigada*

No se le ponga impedimento en su viaje, sino por el contrario, dénsele las mayores facilidades.

P. M. 18 de Diciembre de 1937

El Jefe de E. M.,

Este salvoconducto, caduca el *día de la fecha hasta 18/12/37*

Tip.- Lit. Proletaria U. G. T.- Lérid

A *Salvoconducto* – safe conduct pass – issued to Brigaders on leave, featuring the three-pointed star of the International Brigades. This particular example was issued by the head-quarters of the 13th International Brigade, referred to as Dombrowski, after the Polish national hero. *(RGASPI)*

to desert to the enemy with information about the battalion positions, the other for firing on his comrades with a machine gun while drunk. There exists some suspicion that a handful of others were also executed, the most common offence being desertion. Therefore, the negative political labels assigned to Brigaders during their time in Spain seem to have had limited impact. For example, Sam Wild, who fought with the British battalion through its whole existence, eventually becoming its commander and receiving the Republic's highest award for bravery, is described in the Moscow files as 'weak politically'. Clearly, this judgement did not hold back his military career, nor did it result in incarceration or worse. Instead, Richard Baxell has shown that such files were in fact internal documents that were supposed to assess the value of the volunteers for political work or leadership on their return home, and even the most successful Brigaders were subject to harsh reports. Further, the frequent use of the term Trotskyist is deceptive. Most volunteers would not have known the intricate ideological differences between the Communist Party line and Trotskyism. Instead the term is used in reports to account for a host of problems: drunkenness, disrespect towards officers, pessimism and desertion are all explained as being caused by, or at least developing alongside, Trotskyism or the work of the 'Fifth Column'. Clearly, we should not take this at face value; the majority of these offences were military rather than political, brought about by casualties and defeats. Trotskyism was merely a useful excuse for the disciplinary problems which emerged in the Brigades and the way the term is bandied around in Soviet and Comintern reports suggests that it served as a catch-all term for various problems, the loyal Communist's go-to explanation for any and all ills.

The issue of desertion has been used by some historians to highlight political repression and disaffection within the Brigades; men deserted because they felt oppressed by their Stalinist leaders. Far more logical an explanation is the fact that as the Republic's shock troops, the Internationals fought in an unrelenting series of bloody battles against a better trained and equipped enemy, without much in the way of success or respite. There are few accurate figures available for the rate of desertion, but one Albacete report does tell us that by the end of April 1938, 31,369 foreign volunteers had served in the International Brigades but only 15,992 of them remained; 4,575 had been killed and a further 5,062 badly wounded. The difference, 5,740, has been used by Radosh *et al.* to suggest that thousands of Brigaders must have been executed by the Brigades' repressive disciplinary system or else deserted. This is based on a misreading of the 'sent home' figure in the report, which, at 5,062, is identical to the 'badly wounded' figure and clearly represents only those who were sent home due to combat injuries. An earlier confidential Comintern report of 29 August 1937 helps us understand this discrepancy. This document lists International Brigade losses to date, including 696 disappeared, 1,500 evacuated and 3,287 wounded. Additionally, for the period from April 1937 to the start of August, it lists 4,652 as 'departed abroad'. Evidently, the majority of those who had left were not the badly wounded ('evacuated') and it is well known that in 1937 there was a significant turnover of Brigade personnel; commanders who fell out with the leadership, such as Pacciardi, left Spain, while still others, including veterans of the bloody Madrid battles, were repatriated having 'done their part'. A good example would be the survivors of the British contingents of the Commune de Paris and Thälmann battalions, including Esmond Romilly. Others still were sent home with illnesses unrelated to the war, for instance

Fred Copeman with appendicitis. Therefore, if in just a few months in 1937 as many as 3,000 volunteers departed for a variety of reasons, the 'difference' figure for April 1938 of 5,740 should be seen in a different light. Rather than suggesting that nearly a sixth of the volunteers had either deserted or been executed, as Radosh *et al.* assert, it is far more likely that this figure represents a huge variety of departures, from the disillusioned to the dismissed, to those worn out. Within this number there must be an unknown quantity of deserters and men who were executed, but it seems highly unlikely that these would amount to anything close to the overall figure, especially as we know that more than 3,000 volunteers departed abroad in 1937. The only precise figures we have for desertion are provided by a January 1938 report from 35th Division's commander General Walter. He breaks down the desertion numbers from the 11th International Brigade for October 1937, the month the Republic's Saragossa offensive finally broke down after much hard fighting since August. In total, seventy-two officers and men deserted from the famous 11th Brigade during the month, of whom eighteen were international volunteers and fifty-two were Spanish (at this time, just 14.5 per cent of the 11th's personnel were Internationals, the shortfall being made up with Spanish recruits, including many conscripts). Another example Walter gives is the 15th Brigade, which suffered significant desertions while being transferred from Madrid to Aragon in December 1937, but the Polish general comments 'about 120 men deserted, among whom were internationalists', implying that the large majority once again were Spaniards. He then goes on to set out three instructive cases of deserters brought before the 11th Brigade's military court in November–December 1937. Interestingly (although perhaps not surprisingly given they accounted for more than 85 per cent of the unit) all three defendants were Spanish members of the Brigade:

a) Sergeant José Siles González, thirty-eight years old, member of the CP [Communist Party] of Spain since 1933. Volunteer since 31 August 1936. In the 11th Brigade since 10 April 1937. Was a company commissar. Injured at Brunete. On 17 October 1937 left the brigade without leave, went home, married, and after fifteen days returned. [Siles González was demoted to private, docked a month's pay and spent fifteen days in the penal platoon.]

b) Sergeant Etienne Rovira Leroux, eighteen years old. Volunteer in the brigade since 24 October 1936. Promoted to sergeant on 1 May

1937 for distinguished military service. On 26 November 1937 he got drunk and refused to serve, declaring (not for the first time) that he couldn't take it any longer and didn't want to stay in the brigade and that he was going to Albacete to request a transfer to another International Brigade. [Rovira was demoted to private and given fifteen days in the penal platoon on half pay.]

c) Rafael Lores Cucales. In the brigade as a volunteer since 19 November 1936. Received a ten-day leave and overstayed it by twelve days because of his wife's sickness. The tribunal refused to thoroughly investigate the 'personal' motive for his overstay and simply demoted him to private, sending him for correction to a penal platoon for two weeks.[6]

While Walter rails against the harshness of the sentences in his report, arguing that a 'friendly half-hour conversation' could have resolved the issues, the relatively light sentences make surprising reading considering the reputation of the International Brigades as a brutal organ of Stalinist repression. We lack any solid evidence that desertion was driven by political dissatisfaction and have even less that it was routinely punished with execution. It would therefore be reasonable to conclude that while the Brigades were not lenient by any stretch, the volunteers were not the 'heroic victims' of totalitarianism, both from the enemy and from their own side, that they have sometimes been labelled. Military crimes such as desertion and disrespecting officers were certainly punished, sometimes harshly, particularly at times of crisis, such as the summer of 1937 or the spring of 1938, but this is not unique to the Brigades, with militaries throughout history deeming that it was necessary to act cruelly in certain circumstances, particularly in the wake of routs or defeats, in order to maintain discipline.

The International Brigades were, on the whole, poorly trained. The standard of training throughout the People's Army was certainly low, and it could be argued that most Brigaders actually received more instruction than the average Republican solider, not that that would have been much succour to volunteers at the time. During the early days of the International Brigades, training consisted of little more than a few days of parade drill, manoeuvres and some military basics. Not all volunteers were lucky enough to even fire a rifle before being sent to the front, and for those who did there was precious little ammunition to spare. As the Nationalists threatened to first storm, then encircle Madrid, every

PT for new recruits. (*Tamiment Library and Robert F. Wagner Labor Archive*)

available man was rushed to the front. The experience of the volunteers of the Thälmann battalion in November 1936 was typical of this period:

> At eleven o'clock we marched through the little town to a piece of flat ground in the hills above ... When we halted, Jeans told us that we were going to practise various manoeuvres, that one of the officers present had been a colonel in the Reichswehr [army of Weimar Germany], that he would teach us the very latest German army tactics.
>
> A difficulty soon cropped up, that it appeared he was the only man who knew them. The secret of it all was the triangular arrow-shaped formation – the battalion would be split like this, for attacking, then the companies and so on down to units of three. There was another division as well – out of each group of ten, half would be a light-machine-gun squad, and the rest would be in advance of the squad protecting it with rifle fire. We practised for an hour or two at these manoeuvres.
>
> 'What about enemy tanks?' asked somebody. 'Get as close to them as possible!' was the answer.
>
> The 'manoeuvres' (which always broke down because of bad co-ordination and because we could never understand the general plan)

stopped abruptly when a motorcyclist arrived at breathless speed to give a message to Max. Max told us:

'I am sorry. I wanted all of you to have a thorough training, for sixteen days at least. I am sorry. We are leaving at once for the front (cheers interrupted him at this point). You will go in lorries. We do not know where the enemy is. If the lorries stop, get out at once, go into the nearest house, and stand ready.'[7]

The first International Brigaders had to learn the lessons of modern war the hard way. That being said, the worker and peasant militiamen had no training to speak of and often refused to dig trenches. Even the nascent People's Army units created in the autumn and winter of 1936 had no more than a few days' marching and drill under their belts before they were rushed to the desperate defence of the capital. Therefore, in a time of crisis, all Loyalist troops were in the same boat. As the threat of imminent defeat receded in the spring of 1937, more time could be taken over the training of new recruits. Usually, Brigaders received up to ten weeks' training, including instruction in the use of various weapons and lectures from Brigade veterans on various aspects of modern warfare. Even then, it must be said that such courses continued to prove inadequate, evidenced by the horrendous losses suffered by green units such as the George Washington battalion or the 150th International Brigade at the Battle of Brunete in July 1937. This led to a thorough reorganisation of training at the International Brigade base in Albacete, as was explained by General Goméz in a report to the Comintern:

> Training at the base was completely reorganized. A training battalion was organized for each brigade as well as a training group for the artillery ...
>
> The school for officers at Poco Rubio was reorganized along new lines. Only comrades who had already been present at the front in the rank of officer were permitted to be students. Each course lasted two and a half months. A program based on the one at the military school in Valencia was established.
>
> In every training battalion special schools for sergeants and corporals were organized, and furthermore, special short-term courses for the best marksmen, sighters, and also for work with heavy and light machine guns. For all of these cadres and for the general training of the recruits, a precise, uniform program was established.

At the end of November 1937, six training battalions were organized at Fuente Albilla as the basis for the 12th Brigade, which was being formed that same month. The success of this reorganization manifested itself in the fact that the number of comrades sent to the front each month increased significantly.

During this third stage, that is, from 1 August to 15 November 1937, the average number of comrades sent to the front rose to 2,223. There is no doubt that the training these comrades received was better and more thorough in comparison to the preceding periods.[8]

The seriousness with which the Brigades took the issue of training is illustrated by the fact that the nominally Canadian Mackenzie-Papineau battalion was founded in June 1937 but not sent to the front until September, nor was it deployed in action until October, a grace period that was unheard of just a year before. Their intensive training led to them resembling a more conventional military to a greater extent than the veteran units in their Brigade; for instance, they began the day with a bugle being blown and a roll call. Admittedly, their first combat, like that of almost all the International Brigade units, was a bloody baptism of fire, but with the caveat that it was part of a particularly poorly planned wider operation at Fuentes de Ebro. After this initial shock, the battalion performed relatively well, especially at the Battle of Teruel in the winter of 1937/8. Arriving in Spain in January 1938, New Yorker Alvah Bessie's description of the new training regime compares highly favourably to the earlier picture:

Our preparation followed the accepted outlines of infantry training ... the world over. We marched and countermarched to toughen our muscles ... we ran and fell with our rifles, learning how to fall without hurting ourselves or damaging our arms. We practised close-order drill (the Americans never learned to march properly) and we practised infiltration over the terrain – advancing by squads and platoons and sections; seeking cover, advancing, charging. We dug various types of fortifications – foxholes, firing pits, dugouts and trenches, and we learned how to camouflage them. We received instruction in musketry – dry-firing, triangulation, target practice, fire and movement. We learned how to strip and clean our arms and reassemble them, even in the dark. We were taught how to take cover from various types of fire – artillery, machine gun, rifle, airplane. We were shown how to handle every type of arm the infantry was using,

Remarkably crude anti-tank training. (*Tamiment Library and Robert F. Wagner Labor Archive*)

and we were taught how to care for the wounded; and men who felt they had a flair for the more specialized services – first aid, transmissions, topography, scouting, sniping, anti-aircraft and transport – were given an opportunity at these specialities when men were needed.[9]

Bessie also notes that nearly every recruit was granted the opportunity to command during training, in order that the natural leaders could be identified. Necessity forced change once again, however. The final volunteers who arrived from the spring of 1938 did not enjoy the same level of training that their immediate predecessors had done, for from March 1938 the Republic was thrown into crisis once again by a major Nationalist offensive in Aragon that came to be known by the Republicans as the Great Retreats. The urgent need for men curtailed the more developed training programmes and resulted in new recruits, including Bessie himself, being unceremoniously shipped off to the front early. As the Republic was split in two by Franco's advance to the sea in April 1938, the Albacete base was dismantled and the International Brigades' HQ was re-established in Catalonia, where most of the Internationals were cut off. Practically the only replacements that then arrived were foreign volunteers combed from service arms such as the auto park, deserters forced back to the front, and, in the main, new Spanish conscripts. The People's Army conscripts were generally unmotivated and poorly trained, many having less than a month between receiving their papers and being sent to the front. As a result, throughout the existence of the International Brigades, the men were for the most part too poorly trained to be able to execute complex tactical manoeuvres. This was on the whole the result of necessity and the paucity of the Republican People's Army, in terms of men, equipment and experienced officers and NCOs who could actually oversee meaningful instruction courses. That being said, at least most Brigaders did have more training, however scant, than the average Loyalist militiaman or conscript they were fighting alongside.

The International Brigades were not, as should now be clear to the reader, a typical army of the twentieth century. They were an improvised, polyglot force of idealists and activists, mostly, as with any army, working-class men, but, unusually, inspired by a political commitment to a foreign cause. The training, weapons and equipment of the Brigades were inadequate, and their commanders were not, on the whole, particularly experienced or tactically aware. In turn, the tactics and doctrine of the Brigades were amateurish, even non-existent, and they lacked the firepower to compensate for their lack of guile. In spite of all that, it must be said that the formation of the Brigades was an achievement in itself and the fact that the International Brigades did often prove to be very effective in combat highlights the astounding commitment of so many volunteers to the Republic's cause. The Spanish Civil War has been described as a 'poor man's war', fought by two sides lacking modern weaponry and tactics, with unenthusiastic conscripts making up the vast majority of both

Rare photograph of a trial of International Brigade deserters, October 1937. (*Tamiment Library and Robert F. Wagner Labor Archive*)

armies. It was in this context that the International Brigades could become elite shock troops – they were poorly trained and equipped, but so was the entire Republican army. What made them stand out from the average People's Army mixed brigade was that the volunteers of the International Brigades could be relied upon. They would fight hard in attack or defence, as they would be asked to do, time and again, throughout their brief existence. There can be little dispute that the International Brigades were a 'Comintern Army' in the sense that they were organised, funded and largely recruited by the Communist International. However, they were not merely minions of Moscow, for the diversity of men in the ranks of the International Brigades, united above all else by their opposition to fascism, ensured they were so much more than a Communist legion. They were anti-fascist warriors of all creeds, colours, religions and politics, history's greatest example of international Socialist solidarity. Their experience in Spain was to be, for many, the most trying of their lives.

Chapter 2

Baptism of Fire
November 1936–February 1937

To the Front

Despite Brigade leader André Marty's vow that the international volunteers would go into battle well trained and equipped, military necessity intervened. Just days after the creation of the first International Brigades, the 11th and 12th, these green units would be thrown into one of the war's bloodiest battles of attrition – the siege of Madrid. Since August 1936 Franco's force of elite colonial troops of the Spanish Army of Africa had been rampaging across southern Spain, sweeping aside the ragtag workers' and peasants' militias and Loyalist conscript and police units. The tactics of these units is described well by the American journalist John T. Whitaker, who was with the advancing Nationalists:

> Marching with these Moors, I watched them flank, dislodge, and annihilate ten times their numbers in battle after battle. Individual heroism among untrained soldiers is not enough against professionals supported by aircraft. The Republicans used to fight stubbornly until they could no longer stand under the fragmentation bombs and the artillery fire ... then the Moors would charge and dislodge them from the relative security of their trench systems. With no professional officers and no training ... the beaten Republicans would mill into some village, rushing madly for the illusionary protection of stone houses.[10]

In late September Franco diverted his advance on Madrid to take Toledo, freeing the beleaguered garrison of the famous Alcázar fortress. However, resistance was already hardening, with numerous counter-attacks being launched by the new Republican Under-Secretary for War General Asensio Torrado. Although these efforts failed to push the Nationalists back and were generally marred by the incompetence of both the new Republican commanders and the untrained militiamen, the increasingly

Enemy: Army of Africa

The pre-war Spanish army was divided into two distinct components: the Peninsula or Metropolitan Army based in Spain and the Army of Africa stationed in Spain's Moroccan protectorate. The Peninsula troops were almost exclusively conscripts who lacked training or motivation and generally had little or no combat experience. Meanwhile, the Army of Africa was the elite, representing the most experienced, disciplined, well equipped and motivated troops in the Spanish military. It consisted of around 30,000 men, many of them veterans of the long, bitter Rif War in Morocco (1909–26). There also existed a brutalised proto-fascist military culture in the Army of Africa which ensured that unlike their divided Peninsula colleagues, the colonial forces were firmly behind the Nationalist uprising of July 1936. Africanistas, as they were known, were themselves composed of two distinct elements, the Foreign Legion and the *Regulares*. The Spanish Foreign Legion, while modelled on its French counterpart, was in fact overwhelmingly Spanish in composition. Calling themselves the 'Bridegrooms of Death', the Legionnaires were shock troops whose record of brutality and war crimes had earned them an infamous reputation. Whipping was used as a punishment for cowardice, but the troops enjoyed the swagger and confidence endowed by their status as an elite; indeed, they were paid twice as much as regular Nationalist troops. The *Regulares*, meanwhile, were Moroccan mercenaries with Spanish officers, and

Moroccan *Regulares* with Spanish officers, 1910s.

An infamous photo of Spanish Foreign Legionnaires during the Rif War, where they earned a reputation for mutilating their enemies and taking body parts as prizes.

were perhaps the most feared members of Franco's army. In total, around 78,500 Moroccans were recruited to fight in the civil war; their infiltration and encirclement tactics and their track record of murder, rape and pillage in the campaign in southern Spain meant that Republican troops often fled in the face of the 'Moors'. In the civil war's early months, up to the spring of 1937, Army of Africa troops were deployed together in columns or brigades. Later, they were split up and integrated into various Nationalist divisions, although many colonial troops were concentrated in the Moroccan Corps and the 13th Black Hand Division.

fierce resistance was taking its toll on the outnumbered Rebels. By the time Nationalist forces reached the outskirts of Madrid at the start of November, they could muster an assault force of just 10,000 men, already worn out by several months' continuous fighting.

Nevertheless, in expectation of the immediate fall of the capital, the Republican government fled hastily to Valencia on 6 November, leaving General José Miaja at the head of a defence junta. Although he had 13,000 men at his disposal, with another 10,000 in reserve, most were untrained militia, while 25 per cent of the defence force was made up of paramilitary police units. Miaja was an old but inexperienced officer who had never commanded more than a regiment in combat, yet he, and more significantly his chief of staff, the youthful and energetic Colonel Vicente Rojo, as well as Soviet advisers and equipment, would pull off a seemingly

Franco's Moroccan *Regulares* advance through southern Spain, summer 1936. (*Bundesarchiv*)

miraculous defence of the capital. Stalin had only committed to supporting the Republic in mid-September, when, with the Axis-backed Nationalists on the brink of victory, Soviet policymakers perceived a serious strategic threat to France, their only concrete ally in a projected future conflict with Nazi Germany. They also held hopes that Britain and France would at some point come to the Republic's aid, and that cooperating with these powers in Spain could lead to a comprehensive collective security arrangement against the fascist powers. Despite the eventual frustration of these schemes, in the autumn of 1936 the Soviets dispatched tanks, aircraft, weapons and hundreds of advisers to assist the Republic, the only major power to do so. While Soviet aid would be outstripped in quality by the Germans and in quantity by the Italians, it would prove vital to continued Loyalist resistance.

For the assault on Madrid, Franco placed his most talented general, José Enrique Varela, in command of operations and gave him five columns, each roughly the strength of a brigade, consisting of a Bandera (battalion) of the Foreign Legion, several Tabors (half-battalions) of Moroccan *Regulares*, an artillery battery and support troops. The assault began on 7 November, with a narrow Nationalist salient being driven into the huge Casa de Campo park on the city centre's western edge. Dogged resistance

Nationalist troops pose for propaganda photos during the advance on Madrid.
(*reproduced from Cardozo, 1937*)

The Republican militias, formed by political parties and unions and armed by the government, lacked the skill, equipment and discipline to halt the Rebel advance. (*RGASPI*)

from the Republican militias meant that by 13 November the insurgent advance had stalled on the Manzanares river and in the working-class Carablanchel district. With the very existence of the Republic seemingly under threat, and many media outlets around the world announcing Franco's final triumph, the 11th International Brigade had been rushed to Madrid to aid in the defence on the 8th. Under the command of Red Army intelligence officer General Kléber (real name Manfred Stern), the Brigade, which consisted at this point of 1,900 men of the German Edgar André, French Commune de Paris and Polish Dombrowski battalions, had undertaken a futile counter-attack against the Garabitas hill within the Casa de Campo on 13 November, suffering numerous casualties, before settling in to defensive positions along the Manzanares at the key Bridge of the French. The entry of this first International Brigade into Madrid has become a famous historical episode, with numerous accounts of the war claiming the populace mobbed the marching volunteers, giving them a heroic welcome in a morale-boosting moment that changed the course of

Territorial division of Spain by September 1936, after Franco's rapid advance. Republican-held territory is dark, Nationalist light. (*Wikimedia User Nordnordwest, CC BY-SA 3.0*)

General José Enrique Varela (*seated*), Franco's best general and commander of the assault on Madrid. (*reproduced from Cardozo, 1937*)

the battle. In fact, this version seems to be the product of over-imaginative journalism (the battle was the world's biggest news story at the time) and Communist propaganda. Instead, and perhaps unsurprisingly, their arrival into the besieged city was rather more understated and grim, as one soldier in the Commune de Paris battalion remembered:

> Ours was no triumphant entry; we were a last, desperate hope, and as, tired out, ill-equipped and hungry, we marched through the windswept streets, past the shuttered shops and the food queues, I thought that the hurrying people on the pavements looked at us as if we were too late and had come only in time to die.[11]

Meanwhile, the even more unprepared 12th International Brigade (1,550 men of the German Thälmann, Italian Garibaldi and French André Marty battalions) also fought their first action on 13 November, a hopelessly incompetent counter-attack against another height, the well fortified Cerro de los Ángeles, some 10 kilometres south of Madrid. Supported by a company of Russian T-26 tanks, the three battalions attempted to encircle the position, but with artillery destroying two of the tanks, machine guns firing across open country and troops for the most part not just experiencing combat for the first time but also having never been on manoeuvres, the attack soon fell apart. By nightfall many men, and in some cases entire units, were hopelessly lost and it took several days for the Brigade to reorganise itself and form a proper line, all the while tangling with Moroccan troops in night raids.

University City

After this inauspicious start, the International Brigades were to fight one of their most decisive actions. On 15 November Varela shifted the focus of the Nationalist advance to the newly built (in parts still under construction) University City on the edge of the Case de Campo, across the Manzanares from the park. If the campus could be secured, the path into the Western Park, and then the city centre, would be clear. The heavily fortified lines along the river could be circumvented and the Nationalists could push swiftly on to the Plaza de España and central Madrid. On the morning of 15 November the 11th Brigade's Edgar André and Dombrowski battalions, along with Spanish Communist troops of Romero's battalion, bore the brunt of attacks by Colonels Barrón and Delgado Serrano's columns of colonial troops, supported by German Panzer Is, as they pushed to try to cross the Bridge of the French and several smaller bridges either side of it. As well as using German tanks, the attack was supported by a bombing raid from Hitler's nascent Condor Legion, flying the famous Junkers Ju 52, reportedly the first time German air power had

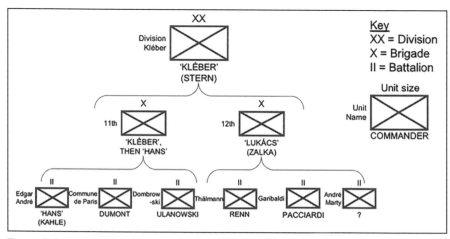

Figure 5. International units at the battle of Madrid, November 1936.

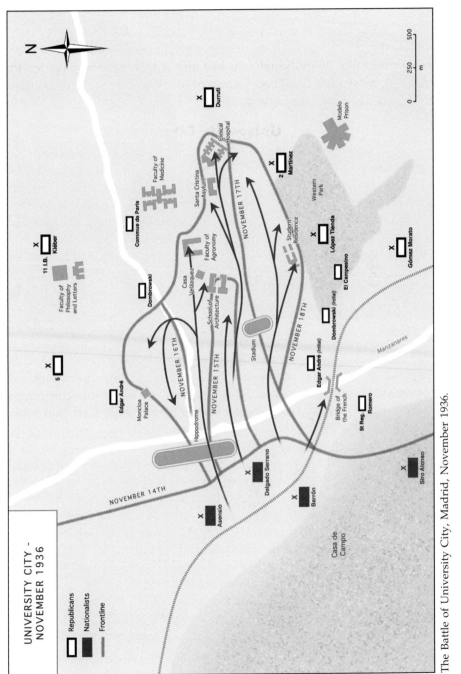

The Battle of University City, Madrid, November 1936.

The Bridge of the French today, so-called because it was built by French engineers. This was the scene of the initial Nationalist push over the Manzanares on 15 November 1936.

been used in the battle. By noon, the bridges had been blown and it appeared that the Rebel assault was running out of steam. The break-through came that afternoon about a kilometre north of the bridges and was achieved by Colonel Delgado Serrano's Column No. 3. On their third attempt to cross the Manzanares, Moroccan troops of the 2nd and 3rd Tabores of Alhucemas waded across the river under fire and burst through a breach blown in the river's walled embankment, causing the Catalan Anarchists of the Durruti Column to flee. Troops from Asensio's 6th Bandera of the Foreign Legion quickly rushed into the open campus, seizing the stadium and the School of Architecture, with some *Regulares* reportedly getting as far as the Faculty of Philosophy and Letters by the end of the day. A pontoon bridge was erected, which would provide a narrow lifeline for the Rebel forces in the University for the duration of the battle, coming under constant fire and making the bringing-up of supplies and the withdrawal of casualties extremely difficult. One group of Moroccans was forced to eat rabbits and rats they found in the labora-tories, only to fall ill from the various diseases the animals had been inoculated with.

General Kléber reacted quickly to the crisis, moving his Internationals overnight from their positions south of the campus in order to seal the breach and prevent them being outflanked by the Nationalist incursion. The French Commune de Paris battalion plugged what Kléber described as a 'gaping hole' in the line, taking back the Philosophy and Letters building swiftly at bayonet point and occupying the Faculty of Medicine, opposite the Casa Velázquez, a French-language college. The Eastern European Dombrowski battalion was transferred from the blown Manzanares bridges to the right of the French volunteers, with a front running from the Casa Velázquez up to the German Edgar André battalion positioned on the northern edge of the Rebel salient, based in the Palace of Moncloa and its various annexes and farmhouses (today the official residence of the Spanish Prime Minister), which overlooked the river crossings and the campus. Kléber himself moved his HQ to the Puerta de Hierro golf club a few kilometres north of University City and, as the battle developed, through improvisation, a lack of other trained officers and sheer force of personality, he took command of the entire sector and its various units (including the 12th International Brigade) which were quickly rushed to

The gigantic Faculty of Medicine in University City today, viewed from the south-east. This image provides an idea of both the scale and the sturdy construction of the campus buildings fought over in 1936. (*Wikimedia user Merkun6, CC BY-SA 4.0*)

the breach, operating under the auspices of a loose 'Division Kléber'. At dawn on the 16th the colonial troops pushed forward again with the Republican defences still taking shape. They seized the Casa Velázquez, all but wiping out the Polish company guarding it, and then advanced into the vast array of medical buildings that amounted to a small suburb, taking the Asylum of Santa Cristina and soon moving into the enormous, seven-storey Clinical Hospital. John Sommerfield was part of a small British contingent within the Commune de Paris battalion, holding the line at the Faculty of Medicine for a number of days, sniping at the Rebel troops in the Casa Velázquez:

> Sometimes there was a movement behind a window across the way, sometimes a figure ran and tumbled and lay still. That was mostly how you killed men in a war; there was a movement and you fired and the movement stopped ... it was impersonal, clay pigeon shooting; you did not think that you were making widows and orphans ... we stared out at them for so many hours that we were familiar with every detail of the scene, every shell-hole in the buildings, every bush and stunted tree on the ground.[12]

At the Clinical Hospital Durruti rallied his Anarchist militia and a long, bitter battle would drag on for the best part of week for this single structure, eventually costing the revolutionary his life. On 17 and 18 November the Nationalists widened their narrow salient both south towards the Western Park and the Modelo Prison and north towards the Moncloa Palace. Asensio's column launched a ferocious attack on the Moncloa complex, with the Polish Dombrowskis bearing the brunt of the assault. Looking down on the Casa Velázquez from the north-west, this quaint complex was made up of small farmhouses, stables, ponds, undulating wooded valleys and banks, as well as the palace itself. In desperate fighting, which Kléber described as 'the most terrible combat episode' of the whole battle, the Rebels managed to seize the Palace:

> The Polish battalion clashed with the Moroccans with hand grenades and bayonets. A terrible fight took place on the stairways and floors of the building. Of the sixty men in a Polish company, one platoon of which was Bulgarians and Yugoslavs, only five or six men were left alive. The battalion commander ... shot himself.[13]

During the afternoon of the 18th the Dombrowski and Edgar Andre battalions of the 11th Brigade began to be relieved, literally in the midst of combat, by arriving troops from the Garibaldi and Thälmann battalions of the 12th Brigade. Meanwhile, the André Marty battalion relieved its French counterparts in the Commune de Paris at the Medical School. That same day, in expectation of Madrid's imminent fall, Germany and Italy recognised Franco's regime as the legitimate government of Spain, the first nations to do so. At dawn the following morning, as the Thälmanns prepared for a counter-attack on the Palace compound, they were informed of this news and told their actions 'would have a decisive effect on the future of international relations'. With this exhortation ringing in their ears, the Thälmann battalion moved against the farm buildings while the Garibaldis attempted to retake Moncloa itself. The Internationals suffered heavy losses from withering machine gun and artillery fire and by noon had been compelled to withdraw, having reached only a few of the annex buildings. Again, on the 20th, the Thälmanns pushed into the farm itself. Esmond Romilly, the teenage tearaway nephew of Winston Churchill, was a volunteer in the German battalion and described what happened as they moved forward, covered by fire from four T-26 tanks and the Garibaldis:

> We reached the wall of the White House. It was a mad scramble ... some of the Germans dropped on the way – it was just like seeing people killed running in an American film ... Most of the fire came from the red house. Outside the wall were the bodies of Moorish soldiers – some still groaning. Machine guns from the clinic hospital [*sic*; in fact the Faculty of Medicine where the French internationals were based] were taking a deadly toll of the defenders. No one could escape by the road behind.[14]

The German volunteers managed to break into the farm complex but at such a cost that they were forced to abandon their gains in the evening, pulling back to the road running down into the campus. The Thälmann battalion held a line from this road leading north from the edge of the University, looking onto the Casa Velázquez, up through a few of the farm buildings, while to their right the Garibaldis held a line along a ridge in the palace complex, down to the Manzanares basin. Over the coming days the Internationals would fight bloody, futile, back and forth battles with the Rebel colonial troops, farm buildings known as the 'Red' and 'White' houses changing hands, but not the palace itself, despite repeated attacks by the Italian volunteers. Casualties were extremely heavy; the Thälmann

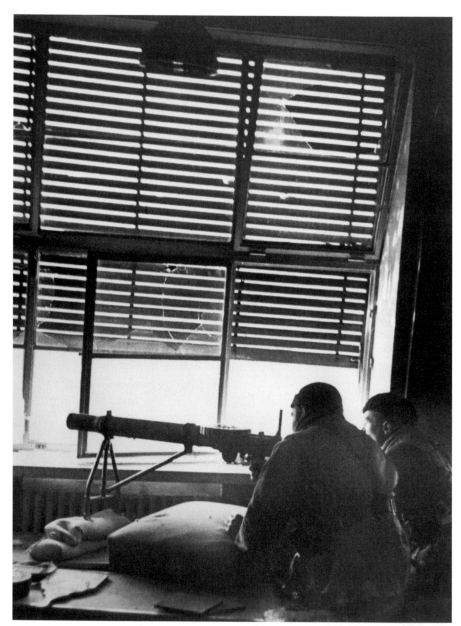

International Brigaders with a Lewis gun, firing from a university building. The right-hand gunner is wearing a leather trench jerkin. This startling photograph gives a real sense of what the combat in the campus was like.

(© *Robert Capa* © *International Center of Photography/Magnum Photos*)

The restored Palace of Moncloa, which today serves as the official residence of the Prime Minister of Spain. During the University City battle it was completely destroyed.
(Flickr user ecemaml CC BY-SA 2.0)

battalion lost over a hundred men, with nearly all the platoon and company commanders among the dead and wounded.

By the 21st the Nationalist attack had ground to a halt. There were only about 2,000 tired and hungry Rebel troops in the entire University City bridgehead; not only were they vastly outnumbered by the defenders, they were vulnerable to constant artillery and machine-gun fire. On 23 November a conference of Franco's leading generals decided that a frontal attack on Madrid was no longer a viable option; instead the capital was to be isolated and forced into surrender. The lines established in the campus would remain practically the same for the duration of the war. The 12th International Brigade held its positions until 27 November, before being relieved by the 11th. Both units had suffered extreme losses in their first combats, fighting bitter house-to-house and room-to-room battles with the finest troops in the Nationalist army. During their first four weeks in action, the 11th suffered 900 casualties and the 12th 750 (from initial strengths of 1,900 and 1,550 respectively), yet their sacrifice had helped to rescue a seemingly desperate situation. While it would be an exaggeration to say the International Brigades saved Madrid (they

Brigadistas: Hans Kahle and the German volunteers

Hans Kahle, referred to simply as Hans during the civil war in order to protect his relatives in Germany, was born in 1899 into a family of Prussian civil servants. He was sent to a military academy before becoming a junior officer and serving on the Western Front in the First World War. In the words of Herbert Matthews of the *New York Times*,

> He fought well. But what he saw then made him hate nationalism, and he became a journalist for radical newspapers. In the struggle against Hitler he was on the losing side and had to leave Germany.
>
> (Matthews, 1938, p. 213.)

Kahle was a leading figure in the exiled German Communist party and had organised aid for the Spanish Asturias revolt of 1934 before assisting in the creation of the International Brigades in 1936. He commanded the Edgar André battalion of the 11th International Brigade, named after a German Communist who was executed by the Nazis just days before the battle of Madrid. When General Kléber took over the University City sector, he promoted Kahle to the rank of lieutenant colonel and appointed him head of the 11th Brigade, which would eventually become known as the *Thälmann* once Austrian and

Richard Staimer (*left*); Mikhail Koltsov, Soviet journalist and Stalin's eyes and ears in Spain (*centre*); and Hans Kahle (*right*).

German volunteers from other brigades were concentrated under his command, with renowned author Ludwig Renn as his chief of staff. The German antifascists gained a reputation from Madrid onwards as some of the toughest and most soldierly of the International volunteers, and other nationalities respected the fact that so many had fought Hitler's brownshirts and would have no home to return to once the war in Spain was over. Some had even survived periods in Dachau and Sachsenhausen. Despite being wounded in January 1937, the following April revealed the high regard in which Kahle was held by Republican leaders when he was appointed commander of the 17th Division, a majority Spanish unit. In September he succeeded Kléber once again, this time as commander of an International unit, the 45th Division. Kahle retained this position throughout the war and the division performed well until the demobilisation of the volunteers in the autumn of 1938. Kahle eventually found his way to Britain, where, after a short spell in internment, he took up journalism and activism once again. In 1946 he was able to finally return to his homeland, becoming a police chief in East Germany, only to die just a year later aged 48.

represented a relatively small percentage of the Republican forces), their steadfastness and willing sacrifice had ensured that a crisis was averted on 15–17 November as the Rebels came tantalisingly close to central Madrid. First World War veteran Gustav Regler, the commissar of the 12th International Brigade, later wrote proudly of the stand the German anti-fascists had made:

> My volunteers displayed an indifference to danger which I find it hard to explain … Out of the uncertainty of the military situation there grew the certainty of gladiators … Most of them were *emigres* who for three years had suffered humiliation at the hands of the Paris, Prague and Swiss police. Some had been obliged to report daily … and apply for another day's asylum. Now they had arms in their hands and a city to defend. The constant threat of death … had restored their dignity. Many were Jews, and their bullets in the darkness were aimed at Hitler.[15]

In command, the controversial figure of Kléber had clearly inspired confidence in his men through his presumed military prowess, his cool temperament and his ability to get things done. To give an example, the English group with the Commune de Paris battalion had been issued hopeless French St Etienne machine guns. They complained to Kléber that

International Brigaders fighting in the University City sector, November–December 1936. This photograph may have been taken amongst the small farm buildings within the Moncloa complex that no longer exist. The soldiers are using Pattern 14 Enfield rifles, likely bought by the Republic on the black market.
(© *Robert Capa* © *International Center of Photography/Magnum Photos*)

Members of a German machine-gun company pose with their Maxim M1910 in Casa de Campo park, Madrid, November 1936. (*Bundesarchiv*)

The Thälmann battalion, and German volunteers more widely, were amongst the most dedicated of the Brigaders and fought extremely hard at University City.
(*David Seymour/Magnum Photos*)

Commander: Emilio Kléber

General Kléber was a Soviet military intelligence agent dispatched to Spain to take command of the International Brigades. Born Manfred Stern, he came from the Bukovina region of the Austro-Hungarian Empire, today an area divided between Romania and Ukraine. Stern was of Jewish descent and studied at Vienna University before being called up in the First World War. Captured on the Eastern Front, he found himself in Russia during the 1917 revolution and was converted to Bolshevism, joining the Red Army in the Russian Civil War. During a long career with the Soviet military, he served as an adviser to Mao's Chinese Red Army from 1932 to 1935 before arriving in Spain in the autumn of 1936. Here, he adopted the *nom de guerre* Kléber (after a French revolutionary general) and claimed to be a Canadian citizen in order to mask direct Soviet intervention in the conflict. Taking command of the first International Brigade, the 11th, he saw action in the battle for Madrid in November 1936, winning great prestige for his role in the defence of the city, being appointed a sector commander and even being labelled by some foreign journalists the 'Saviour of Madrid'. This merely served to gain Kléber the ire of both Spanish and Comintern colleagues and accusations of 'Kléberism' – the habit of claiming all the credit for oneself. Due to such political machinations he was relieved of his command in January 1937, but was reinstated to head the new 45th Division following the death of General Lukács. By the autumn of 1937 he had once again been dismissed from command, this time for good following perceived failures at Brunete and Belchite. Upon his return to the USSR he fell victim to Stalin's purges and spent the rest of his life in a Siberian gulag, dying in 1954. Kléber was a cool, capable commander who inspired confidence in the rookie Brigaders and was able to elicit from them supreme levels of sacrifice, reminiscent of the better First World War generals. For Hemingway, he was a 'good soldier', who had done 'a fine job', while Herbert Matthews described him as 'the man of the hour' during the Madrid battle.

they should be re-equipped with Lewis machine guns, a weapon that the servicemen among them knew well. Kléber promised he would see what he could do and on their arrival in Madrid, his promise was fulfilled as eight Lewis guns appeared, leaving the group 'delighted, full of kind feelings for Kléber'. While some have criticised Kléber as an unimaginative leader, no better than a tough First World War commander according to Beevor, it is hard to imagine what more he could have achieved leading what amounted to, at least in the winter of 1936, a polyglot militia with a hodgepodge of weapons and equipment and practically no training. To have elicited the combat performance and fighting spirit he did from the Internationals – mirroring the best First World War troops in their determination in attack and defence (and indeed their casualty rates) – Kléber must be credited with pulling off an extraordinary feat. Despite this, his personal prestige produced ire among his Spanish comrades and Comintern officials, and political machinations led, in January 1937, to the Red Army officer being removed from command for a time.

Winter Battles

However, the threat to Madrid had not been averted. On 14 December Varela's reorganised forces, attacking amidst a dense fog, stormed the village of Boadilla de Monte, north-west of the city, but were prevented from advancing much further over the following days by the 11th and 12th International Brigades, who suffered enormous casualties. To try to distract the Nationalists from the capital, a series of counter-attacks were

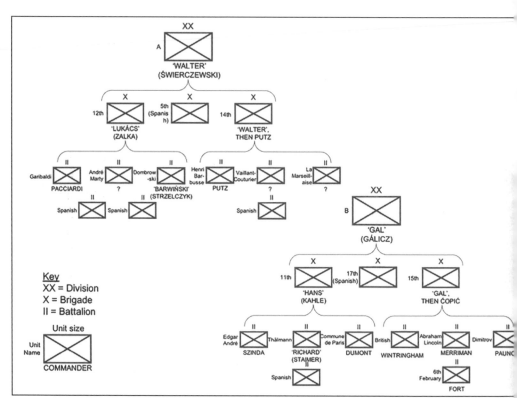

Figure 6. International units at the battle of Jarama, February 1937.

Madrid in ruins after the battle. Contemporary propaganda labelled the city the 'Tomb of Fascism'.

Nationalist troops, armed with Spanish Mausers and a Hotchkiss machine gun, on the Bilbao front during Franco's northern campaign. (*Bundesarchiv*)

launched in other sectors, with the newly created 13th and 14th International Brigades being thrown into battle even less prepared than their predecessors. The 13th Brigade, at this stage composed of Eastern Europeans, French and Belgians, was part of a fruitless assault on Teruel, Aragon, while the mostly French *La Marseillaise* 14th Brigade carried out an utterly hapless attack towards Lopera on the southern front in late December, which served only to decimate their own ranks. On 3 January 1937 the Nationalists renewed their offensive in the Boadilla sector with 12,000 men and 40 tanks, advancing by the 9th to the Madrid–Corunna highway, taking Las Rozas and threatening to outflank the Loyalist lines in the Casa de Campo and University City. On 11 January various Republican formations, including the 12th, 13th and 14th International Brigades, supported by Soviet armour, launched a desperate counter-attack, but it achieved little other than to exhaust and deplete both sides. The 14th International Brigade retook Las Rozas with support from Soviet T-26s, but abandoned the village when the tanks withdrew and a second attack the following day to make good their error was a bloody failure. By 15 January the battle was over, the Republicans having suffered 6,775 casualties and

Francoist Foreign Legionnaires at rest at Navalcarnero during the winter battles around the Corunna road. (*reproduced from Cardozo, 1937*)

Men of the Thälmann battalion, 11th International Brigade, at rest in Murcia after the tough fighting around Madrid, early 1937. (*Bundesarchiv*)

4,100 sick, owing to the freezing conditions. The strength of the International Brigades committed to the Corunna battles was reportedly down by a third.

February would see Franco's next attempt to encircle Madrid, this time with an offensive across the river Jarama, south of the city, aimed at seizing the highway linking Madrid with the new Republican capital in Valencia. Bolstered by fresh recruits from Morocco, the Rebel general Luis Orgaz was able to field 18,600 troops in five brigades for his new offensive, launched on 5 February, supported by sixty Panzer Is and more than a hundred artillery pieces. Initially, the battered International Brigades were not involved in the fighting, but as Loyalist forces crumbled and the Nationalists reached the river itself, General Pozas, head of the Republican Army of the Centre, rushed reinforcements to the sector, having been building up troops for an offensive in this area himself. On 10 February, with the 3rd Brigade of Colonel Barrón pushing dangerously close to the river crossings, the André Marty battalion of the 12th International Brigade was deployed to defend the bridges of Arganda and Pindoque. At 3.00am the next morning French sentries on the Pindoque bridge had their throats cut by Barrón's Moroccan troops and the Rebels streamed

Italian volunteers in the Madrid region, December 1936 or January 1937. In the foreground is some form of improvised mortar. (*Imperial War Museum*)

Major Richard Staimer, known in the civil war as 'Richard' or 'Hoffmann', was a German officer in the International Brigades. He replaced Ludwig Renn as commander of the Thälmann battalion, then followed Kahle as commander of the 11th International Brigade, leading that famous unit from April to December 1937. Staimer later rose to the rank of general in the East German army. *(IWM)*

across onto the other side of the Jarama, creating panic and confusion. The 12th International Brigade fell back several kilometres to the height of Pajares and Nationalist cavalry ran riot in the Republican rear. On the night of the 11/12 February Colonel Asensio's 1st Brigade was able to cross the river further downstream and move towards the southern portion of the Meseta hills, just a few kilometres from the Valencia highway. With the Republican lines in a state of disarray, the 11th and 15th International Brigades were thrown into the breach. The 15th had been founded the previous month and was composed of a British battalion, the Balkan Dimitrov battalion and a French-Belgian 6th February battalion (the British battalion had been dubbed Saklatvala after a recently deceased British-Indian Communist MP but the name did not stick). The American Abraham Lincoln battalion was still in training at Albacete, but the brigade as a whole had only had rudimentary preparation for combat, just like their predecessors in the 11th and 12th Brigades before Madrid.

With orders simply to advance towards the river, the Internationals moved across open country; from north to south there were the Commune de Paris, Edgar André and Dombrowski battalions of the 11th Brigade

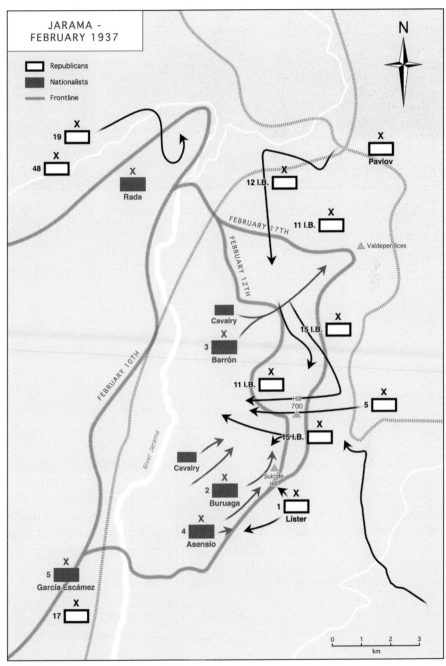

The Battle of Jarama, February 1937.

(*Opposite and above*) Four images illustrating the rugged terrain and rolling hills of the Jarama valley over which the 15th Brigade's first battle was fought.
(*Tamiment Library and Robert F. Wagner Labor Archive*)

A Soviet T-26 of Pavlov's armoured brigade in action in support of the Dimitrov battalion. At first Soviet tanks and aircraft were supplied with crews, but as the war went on Spaniards were trained up to take their place. (*Tamiment Library and Robert F. Wagner Labor Archive*)

and then the Dimitrov, 6th February and British battalions of the 15th. The 11th International Brigade, since Kléber's departure under command of the German Communist Hans Kahle, encountered Barrón's troops, who were themselves reeling from a counter-attack by Soviet armour, and fought robustly. However, further south disaster would strike as the green 15th Brigade ran straight into Moroccan troops of the Rebel 2nd Brigade under Colonel Sáenz de Buruaga, which had crossed the Pindoque bridge after Barrón and moved rapidly south. Attempting to defend a series of rolling hills and knolls, the British battalion was outflanked and utterly decimated by the advancing *Regulares*, with the French and Balkan units also soon retreating desperately for Hill 700 to the north-east, where they linked up with the 11th Brigade. The British meanwhile were saved by their machine-gun company, which, after logistical difficulties, only came into action as the sun was setting. The next evening (13 February) the exposed machine-gunners were overrun by Rebel troops and the British once again retreated in confusion after a failed counter-attack, holding out in a desperately exposed position in a sunken road before being broken again on 14 February by a tank attack. Despite being rallied by their despairing officers and eventually reforming some sort of line late on 14 February, the battalion had been shattered in just three days' combat; from a strength of 500, the British had lost 136 dead and more than 200 wounded, captured or missing. However, by now the main focus of the Rebel advance had shifted north, with Barrón's 3rd Brigade driving the 11th and 12th International Brigades back from Pajares on 13 February, forcing them to withdraw nearly 3 kilometres to a height known as Valdeperdices.

At the same time the Nationalist offensive was running out of steam, due to both stiffening Republican resistance, but more importantly to constant counter-attacks on the peripheries of the Rebel bridgehead. Indeed, Varela's chief of staff would label 14 February 'the Jarama's sorrowful day'. The Dimitrov and 6th February battalions had pushed into Barrón's flank from Hill 700 on 13 February and the 1st Mixed Brigade of the famous militiaman Major Enrique Líster had attacked further south against Asensio's 4th Brigade. Laza Wovicky was a volunteer with the Dimitrovs and he wrote of their counter-attack:

> At 7 o'clock we attacked with the tanks. We drove them back for about a kilometre, but we had to retire to our original positions. None of us were very pleased at leaving the ground we had so well gained … But there was some danger of our being surrounded. Our artillery

French, Belgian and Slavic volunteers of the 15th Brigade in the trenches at Jarama.
(*Tamiment Library and Robert F. Wagner Labor Archive*)

A Moroccan machine-gun team with their Hotchkiss M1914. The *Regulares* proved tough opponents for the 15th International Brigade during their first battles at the Jarama. (*Bundesarchiv*)

bombarded the enemy positions very heavily, and because of this we were able to retire in perfect order ... we were ordered to advance on the left ... but the enemy tanks advanced towards us again, and now we had only our rifles to use against them. We took cover as best we could, but I could see the anger and exasperation of many comrades, as they fired the useless bullets against the steel shells of these moving monsters.[16]

On 14 February fifty T-26s of the Soviet tank brigade rampaged through Sáenz de Buruaga's lines, supported by troops from the 11th and 15th International Brigades and the 5th Mixed Brigade. Additionally, Republican air power was finally making itself felt on the Jarama, with Russian I-16 fighters driving the Axis air forces from the skies. Although these counters failed to push the Rebels back significantly, they drained the momentum from the Nationalist advance and forced the colonial troops onto a defensive footing. With the danger seemingly past, a larger-scale but ultimately pointless counter-offensive began on 18 February aimed at capturing yet another height in the hilly Jarama valley, El Pingarrón, close to the village of Casas de las Siete Villas and some kilometres south of the

(Above) International volunteers manning a Maxim M1910 machine gun in a crude trench at Jarama. The construction of trenches by both sides in the Civil War left much to be desired. (*Tamiment Library and Robert F. Wagner Labor Archive*)

(Left) Major Gabriel Fort, a French socialist and First World War veteran, commanded the French–Belgian 6th February battalion. He was blinded by a bullet at the battle of Brunete and the battalion was disbanded soon after. (*Tamiment Library and Robert F. Wagner Labor Archive*)

Brigadistas: George Nathan and the British and Irish volunteers

George Montague Nathan, born in 1895, was the finest leader among the British volunteers in Spain. Tall, unflappable and Jewish, Nathan had served in the British army before and during the First World War, rising through the ranks to become an officer. After the war he had served in the Anglo-Irish conflict as an auxiliary, associated with the notorious Black and Tans, and was supposedly involved in the murder of the Mayor of Limerick in 1921. Nathan struggled in civilian life and developed vaguely Socialist political views, although he never joined a political party. Arriving in Spain in December 1936, he was made commander of the first proper British unit in the International Brigades, a company of British and Irishmen in the new, largely French, 14th International Brigade. With an adopted officer's accent (he was from a working-class family in Hackney) and immaculate uniform, Nathan inspired confidence in his men with his decisiveness, clarity and arrogance under fire: he was never seen carrying a weapon, only his swagger stick. After the 14th Brigade's disaster at Lopera (where Nathan is credited with saving the lives of many of his men), he was put in command of the French battalion in which the British were serving, before the foundation of the 15th International

George Nathan (*centre*). To his right is another leader of the earlier British contingent, Jock Cunningham, who took over command at Jarama after Wintringham was injured. (*IWM*)

Brigade in January 1937 saw the transfer of the British and Irish to the new British battalion. Nathan was promoted to major and made the 15th Brigade's Chief of Staff. However, the largely Republican Irish volunteers (many of them veterans of the IRA) resented serving in the 'English' battalion, as it was generally referred to, and were outraged by rumours of Nathan's past in Ireland. Effectively put on trial by the Irish contingent, Nathan was forced to explain himself, insisting that they were all on the same side now. Although he appears to have won the Irish over, a number of them soon left for the American Lincoln battalion. Unfazed, Major Nathan's cool confidence at Jarama rallied at various times the Dimitrov, French–Belgian 6th February and British battalions in a number of crises. British commander Captain Tom Wintringham wrote:

> A lean figure with a pipe and walking-stick came swinging down from a hill beside the road. George Nathan ... could be 'spotted' a mile-off by his walk, his bearing, his pipe, stick, British officer's jacket, light-coloured, well-cut breeches. 'Your battalion's a bit late, Tom,' he said, as matter-a-fact as if we had been going to some parade or tattoo.
>
> (Wintringham, 1939, p. 63.)

Ironically, it appears that the volunteers, largely staunch, working-class Communists, were always reassured by the presence in their ranks of a British officer in the traditional mould.

Nathan's luck finally ran out at Brunete in July 1937, when, as the battle drew to a close, he was hit during an aerial bombardment. His death seems to have ended the prospects of an English-speaking officer ever commanding the 15th International Brigade, for even the Soviets regarded him as exceptional.

15th International Brigade's desperate stand. Troops from seven brigades under the direction of Líster, and supported once again by the Soviet T-26s of Pavlov's armoured brigade, made a push for the hill, with the Lísters (1st Mixed Brigade) seizing the summit only to be forced off it by a Moroccan *Tabor* the following day. On 23 February the offensive was renewed, with the height changing hands four times and the 15th Brigade's Lincoln battalion receiving its baptism of fire in a failed attack, achieving an advance of just 600 metres. The tragic final act of the Jarama battle was an utterly futile assault launched by the Lincolns on 27 February. The battalion commander, an economics teacher at Berkeley, Captain Robert Hale Merriman, had begged the 15th Brigade's rather inept Croatian commander Lieutenant Colonel Vladimir Čopić not to launch the attack, sensing the slaughter that was to come. Čopić had insisted it go ahead at

Jarama was the first battle for the Dimitrov battalion, made up of various Balkan volunteers, predominantly Bulgarians, and named after the head of the Comintern.
(*reproduced from Book of XV Brigade*)

all costs and promised air and armoured support that never materialised. Merriman was almost instantly wounded as the attack on the hill quickly faltered:

> About noon the order came to go over the top. The sun was hot. Group by group hopped the trenches charging the Fascists who were only about 250 metres away ... The enemy machine guns began their ugly work ... Soon the calls for First Aid came then became insistent. Many got wounded just as they climbed the parapet to go over. Some comrades from among the recent arrivals, uninformed and inexperienced, went over the top with full packs on their backs and charged towards the Fascists.[17]

In all, 136 Lincolns were killed in this pointless action. Yet the Nationalists had been halted a few kilometres from the Valencia highway (now subjected to intermittent shelling) and suffered 7,900 casualties. Republican losses stood at 7,370 plus 3,300 sick. The International Brigades had been

Disaster: The British stand at Jarama

The first three days of battle for the 15th International Brigade's British bat-talion was the very definition of a baptism of fire. Advancing on 12 February with no maps or intelligence regarding enemy positions or strength, they ran straight into Moroccan troops of the Rebel 2nd Brigade. Taking up positions on a series of small hills (the main one quickly dubbed 'Suicide Hill'), the British attempted to hold the line, their Colt and Chauchat machine guns failing repeatedly. The skilful *Regulares* moved round the exposed left flank of the Internationals' line and also took up positions to the right of the British as the French–Belgian 6th February battalion was compelled to withdraw. Under horrific enfilading fire, Suicide Hill became a death-trap, while the battalion commander, Tom Wintringham, positioned more than a kilometre behind the front with no form of communication with his men, was oblivious to the carnage for several hours. Fred Copeman was one of the volunteers on the exposed hillside:

> Stretcher bearers were going back now in long lines. Kit Conway [an Irish company commander] had got one in the stomach and was obviously not going to live long. Ken Stalker, the commander of No. 2 section, had been wounded. In fact, most of the leadership had gone ... I felt a burning in my hand, and looking down saw that the inside of my watch had gone. There were two holes in my sleeve, and a piece of bullet protruded from my hand. Within seconds the burning became almost intolerable.
>
> (Copeman, 1948, p. 90.)

A chaotic retreat followed, with the Nationalists only halted when the battalion machine-gun company finally opened up, after having been sent the wrong ammunition for their Maxims that morning. The following day, after a panicked withdrawal by one of the rifle companies, the machine-gunners were left isolated and their position was stormed by Foreign Legionnaires. In a desperate attempt to make amends, the guilty company commander led a suicidal charge to retake the trench, only for the British to have their own machine guns turned against them. Just six of the forty men who went over the top returned and Wintringham was wounded. On the third day of the battle the battalion was subjected to a tank attack; lacking any counter-measures, the men were routed, only to be rallied by the 15th Brigade commander as well as the ex-Black and Tan George Nathan and the IRA's Frank Ryan. They gathered 140 men and reformed a line, although historians disagree as to whether there is any truth in the story that their brave singing of the 'Internationale' as they counter-attacked resulted in the Nationalist forces falling back, believing strong reinforcements of fresh troops were being brought up.

thrown into the battles for Madrid without much in the way of training or organisation, frequently facing hardened colonial veterans from the Army of Africa, who, although tactically superior, were usually matched by the Internationals when it came to sheer courage and determination. They had suffered tremendous losses and learnt the lessons of modern warfare the hard way, but they had held their own for the most part. Over the course of the next year the Internationals would become some of the most reliable shock troops of the new Republican People's Army.

Chapter 3

Shock Troops
March 1937–February 1938

Guadalajara

Having survived the numerous assaults on Madrid, the Republic underwent a thorough military and political reorganisation. The International Brigades became an integral part of the newly built People's Army, which would attempt a number of offensives in 1937 and early 1938, with the volunteers often playing a key role. Before this could take place, there was one final act in the siege of Madrid. The Italian *Corpo Truppe Volontarie* (CTV) had been deployed to southern Spain by Mussolini at the turn of the year to assist Franco's Nationalists directly. In February they had led a lightning attack on the poorly defended city of Málaga. Hungry for more triumphs, and deceived into thinking the Republicans defensively inept, the CTV's commander General Roatta rapidly transferred his troops to the Madrid sector, planning an offensive towards Guadalajara which would

Republican troops in a makeshift trench near Malaga, which fell to the Italians in February 1937. The machine gun is a Colt M1895, which often jammed in unfamiliar hands according to Tom Wintringham. (*Bundesarchiv*)

Territorial division of Spain in March 1937, after the Madrid battles. Republican-held territory is dark, Nationalist light. (*Wikimedia User Nordnordwest, CC BY-SA 3.0*)

cut off the city from the north-west. Franco promised a renewed drive on the Jarama to link up with the Fascist Italian push, but he did not keep his word; the troops on the Jarama were reportedly too exhausted.

The 31,200-strong CTV was probably the most mobile fighting force in Spain, consisting of three semi-motorised divisions of Fascist Blackshirt volunteers recruited for the war, and the Littorio Motorised Infantry Division of Italian army regulars, 120 artillery pieces, 46 tankettes and 2,400 trucks. However, the leadership, morale, organisation and motivation of the Italian troops were poor; few were ideologically committed volunteers, the majority of the recruits being peasant farmers or unemployed labourers motivated by no more than the promise of reasonable pay. Many had expected to serve in Abyssinia and were unhappy about being dispatched to Spain. Additionally, as was to become evident in the Second World War, Italian military equipment was generally of a low standard and the rather pathetic CV-33 tankettes they fielded were no match for the Soviet T-26. Despite all these limitations, Roatta's offensive started well enough on 8 March 1937, with two Blackshirt divisions (the 2nd Black Flames and the 3rd Black Feathers) advancing fairly quickly southwards down two main roads bound for Guadalajara and Brihuega. The Republican forces in the sector were decidedly weak. Despite an unseasonal snowstorm and the Italians' lack of winter clothing and equipment, by 10 March they had advanced 30 miles and captured Briheuga. However, the Republicans responded adroitly, quickly rushing in reinforcements which included the new 11th Division under Major Líster (unquestionably the finest unit in the People's Army) and the 14th Division under the capable Anarchist commander Cipriano Mera. A supporting Nationalist push further west made some surprising progress but was eventually contained by the Republican 12th Division, rallied by the appointment of Italian Communist Nino Nanetti as its commander. Additionally, the 11th and 12th International Brigades under Kahle and Lukács, assigned to the 11th and 14th Divisions respectively, played a key role in halting the Italian drive. Two factors outside Roatta's control ensured the operation would fail: Franco's failure to launch an attack in the Jarama sector and the weather. The rain, sleet and snow meant that the Nazi, Italian and

The CTV advances on Guadalajara. (*Bundesarchiv CC BY-SA 3.0 DE*)

Brigadistas: Randolfo Pacciardi and the Italian volunteers

Born in Tuscany in 1899, First World War veteran Randolfo Pacciardi was one of the most highly regarded commanders of the International Brigades. His Garibaldi battalion had arguably the finest reputation of any International unit in the first phase of the war. A lawyer, and leading figure of the Republican party banned by Mussolini, Pacciardi left the comfort of exile in Paris for the trenches of University City and the Jarama. The 12th Brigade commissar Gustav Regler wrote of the Italian's performance in the latter battle:

> Pacciardi was everywhere and master of them all, like a proconsul untroubled by nerves or fear . . . the Garibaldi contingent, composed of all the left-wing parties and possessing in Pacciardi a leader of exceptional intelligence, vigour and understanding, was a well-knit body. They had a quality of true Roman pride. (Regler, 1959, p. 289.)

Wounded at Jarama, Pacciardi could not lead his men during their greatest triumph at Guadalajara, but when his superior officer, the 12th Brigade's General Lukács, was killed at Huesca on 11 June 1937, Pacciardi succeeded him. However, as commander of the 12th International Brigade Pacciardi's star began to wane, his forces failing in the aforementioned Huesca offensive and putting in a decidedly mixed performance at Brunete, resulting in his dismissal. He clashed with the Communists in the Brigades, notably Kléber, over the issue of leave for the Italians and the integration of Spanish troops into International units. Disillusioned, he would eventually leave Spain later that year. Pacciardi himself went on to be Minister of Defence in the post-war Italian Republic, but his Garibaldis would never recapture the fighting spirit displayed under his leadership, with decidedly lacklustre showings at Saragossa and the Ebro, surely also due to the heavy losses of veteran troops.

Nationalist air forces, operating largely from bases north of the Guadarrama mountains, could not reach the battlefield. Meanwhile, the Republican air arm, taking off from airfields much closer, to the south and east of Madrid, was able to intervene heavily in the coming days. Starting on 11 March, a series of massive airstrikes hampered the CTV advance; strung out along two open roads, the Italian motorised columns were hopelessly exposed and soon burning lorries and abandoned equipment

With more than fifty CV 33 tankettes and thousands of trucks, the CTV was probably the most mobile force in Spain. However, the tankettes soon proved to be highly vulnerable to both the Republican T-26 tanks and even machine-gun fire. (*Bundesarchiv CC BY-SA 3.0 DE*)

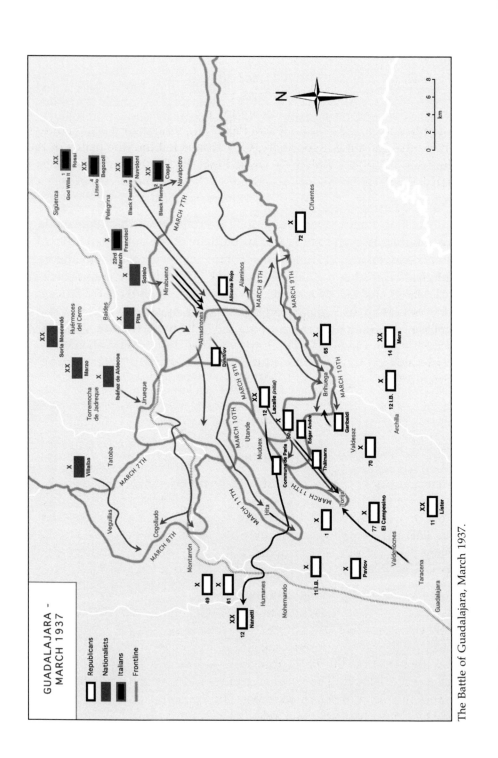

The Battle of Guadalajara, March 1937.

littered the highways, with Italian morale undermined by the threat from the air. Meanwhile, the 11th Brigade had been deployed and was tasked with defending Torija, where the two roads along which the Italians were advancing met, while the 12th, including the Garibaldis, was positioned west of Brihuega, around the Ibarra Palace, fighting their fellow country-men for the first time. Reportedly, CTV troops fell into the hands of the volunteers when they obligingly walked into the Garibaldis' lines, having heard Italian voices and presumed they were friendly troops. *New York Times* reporter Herbert Matthew was at the scene as Mussolini's offensive was halted:

> The enemy came on lickety-split and received their first hard jolt then and there. Ludwig Renn, Han's adjutant [*sic*, Renn was in fact com-missar of Hans Kahle's 11th Brigade] and a strategical expert of con-siderable merit told me ... how revealing that first clash was. Those seasoned veterans immediately realised that the opposing force was not well trained nor being expertly led. The various units were not properly co-ordinated, and they advanced, exposing themselves reck-lessly and without sending patrols far enough forward. Under the circumstances they were naturally jarred on their heels and halted.[18]

The CTV made one last effort on the 11th, the day Loyalist air power really began to make its presence felt, but the Italians' push for Torija was halted by the 11th International Brigade and supporting units from the Lísters. Matthews reported it was the turning point of the battle:

> Hans [Kahle] told me later that he had authority to abandon Torija, but he sensed that the Italian impetus was weakening and decided to hold his ground ... That trip to Torija also convinced me that the Italian force had been definitely stopped – as they deserved to be. They had not only fought badly, but their leaders had let them be locked in an immovable grip with their flanks exposed.[19]

Fierce resistance, combined with the cold and air attacks, seems to have broken the morale of the Fascist troops, for General Roatta felt it necessary to relieve his two lead divisions with those in reserve, the 4th Littorio and 1st God Wills It. This process took several days and only served to throw away the initiative, for the Republicans were now free to prepare a full-scale counter-attack. The counter came on 18 March and the Italian advance was soon transformed into a rout. The Republican 11th, 12th and 14th Divisions, supported by Pavlov's tanks and enjoying air superiority,

After a firm response from the People's Army, the CTV was first halted and eventually driven back, enraging Mussolini. *(Bundesarchiv CC BY-SA 3.0 DE)*

drove the CTV back several miles (although not to their start lines) and retook Brihuega. The International Brigades played a supporting role, advancing quickly to the west of the town, with the honour of liberating it falling to Spanish troops. The Fascists suffered a little under 3,000 casualties and lost a huge quantity of supplies and equipment – 25 artillery pieces, 90 vehicles and over 1,000 small arms. A further 3,719 Italian wounded and sick were returned home. Mussolini was furious and the Internationals had once again played an important role in halting a Nationalist offensive.

The victory at Guadalajara, the Republic's first real triumph, was held up as miraculous and touted by Loyalist propaganda as evidence that the tide had turned. The truth was rather less dramatic. It was a victory, but not an especially decisive one. The main impacts were in fact negative for the Republicans. Firstly, Franco and his generals were finally convinced of the impossibility of taking or surrounding Madrid – the People's Army was too strong in the central zone. Therefore, from late March until October 1937 the main focus for the Nationalists would be the so-called Northern Zone, an isolated Republican enclave on the Cantabrian coast,

Huge quantities of Italian equipment were abandoned in the rout or destroyed in Republican air strikes. Stocks of Italian grenades captured at Guadalajara were still being used by the People's Army in 1938. *(Bundesarchiv CC BY-SA 3.0 DE)*

encompassing the Basque Country, Santander and Asturias. This was a key industrial region but was cut off, largely deprived of Russian equipment and international volunteers, and even more politically divided than the rump of the Republic. Success in the north would prove instrumental in the Nationalists' eventual triumph. Secondly, it convinced Franco's

The Edgar André battalion, 11th International Brigade, at rest in 1937, possibly after Guadalajara. *(Bundesarchiv CC BY-SA 3.0 DE)*

Axis allies that a considerable increase in the scale of their intervention would be required to achieve victory, resulting in an ever-growing supply of German and Italian aid arriving in Spain throughout 1937 as Soviet shipments to the Republicans began to tail off from the spring.

New Army, New Offensives

With a change of government and direction in the spring of 1937, the creation of a regular People's Army was finally achieved by Republican military authorities. The ragtag militias had been – broadly speaking – trained, equipped and reorganised into mixed brigades, divisions, corps and armies in a more traditional, if overly bureaucratic, structure. Augmented with hundreds of thousands of conscripts, this force was to resist the superior Nationalist army for another two years. In 1937, however, the government was keen to go on to the offensive, both to ease the pressure on the Northern Zone, now suffering under the full weight of Axis air power, but also to prove to both domestic and international audiences that the Republic was capable of winning the war. The International Brigades were, along with the finest of the Spanish formations, such as the 11th and 46th Divisions, the crack units of the new People's Army, being far more experienced and battle-hardened than the vast majority of the conscript and militia-based brigades. Up to the spring of 1937 the flow of foreign volunteers had been considerable and, in general, the losses of the winter could be replaced. Additionally, the supply situation in terms of weapons and equipment, although never good, was at least improving and units were much more standardised by mid-1937, versions of the Mosin Nagant rifle and Maxim machine gun being International Brigade staples.

A series of pinprick attacks, aimed at distracting Franco from his northern objectives, were launched in the early summer with the International Brigades playing a supporting role. With the Nationalists closing in on the Basque capital of Bilbao, on 31 May the Republicans launched an attack aimed at capturing Segovia, north-west of Madrid. Three divisions were involved, along with the French-Belgian 14th International Brigade, but the operation was a total failure; by 6 June the Loyalists had been pushed back to their start lines and had suffered 3,000 casualties, including 1,000 from the 14th International Brigade. The Polish divisional commander General Walter argued bitterly with the 14th Brigade's French leader Colonel Jules Dumont over the latter's negligence and inefficiency. His unit had put in decidedly poor performances throughout its short

existence and henceforth would be stationed on quiet fronts, not partici-
pating in any major battles for over a year. Thanks to his high standing
in the French Communist Party, Dumont would not be replaced until
February 1938. Next, the capture of Huesca was attempted, a provincial
capital that formed a narrow Rebel salient in the far north of Aragon. The
divisions in this sector were largely Anarchist and POUM (anti-Stalinist)
in their composition; both groups were reluctant to accept military organisation and authority, and were badly demoralised after the 'May Days'
internal power-struggle in Barcelona, in which their parties had been
forced to climb down, with the POUM eventually being suppressed. Two
International Brigades were to assault from the northern border of the

General Walter examines a Mosin-Nagant rifle issued to his troops. This particular example
is a Dragoon model from the 1920s. (*Tamiment Library and Robert F. Wagner Labor Archive*)

The 14th International Brigade, which failed miserably at Segovia. Its controversial commander Jules Dumont is possibly the figure in the centre, wearing a beret. (*RGASPI*)

pocket, while local Spanish forces would meet them from the south. Labelled the 45th Division, the Internationals were the veteran 12th Garibaldi Brigade and the newly formed 150th International Brigade of Slavic Volunteers, under the overall command of the leader of the former, the Hungarian Red Army officer General Lukács. However, on 11 June, the day before the assault was to commence, Lukács' staff car was hit by a shell, killing the popular commander. The 12th Brigade's commissar Gustav Regler was also in the car and was wounded severely:

> The shell got us just as we were driving past the Anarchist battalions. Our car was lifted into the air, to drop with a thud. I felt a savage blow in the back, and my hands were covered with splintered glass. The driver, beside me, was dead with his hand clutching the brake. The Russian interpreter behind me was leaning forward, motionless. Lukacz [*sic*] was lying with his grey head against the upholstery; his brains were exposed.[20]

French troops of the 14th Brigade in position in the vicinity of Madrid, early 1937.

General Lukács (real name Máté Zalka), Hungarian author and commander of first the 12th International Brigade and then the 45th Division. Zalka had volunteered for the Austro-Hungarian army in the First World War and for the Red Army in the Russian civil war. He was killed by a shell near Huesca in June 1937. *(RGASPI)*

The Garibaldi battalion's Randolfo Pacciardi took over the 12th Brigade, while the hero of Madrid General Kléber was restored to command at the head of the 45th Division, but, only arriving the night before the attack was due to take place, he was not able to familiarise himself with the troops, terrain or enemy positions. He was refused permission to delay the operation and as a result it failed miserably; Republican forces achieved an advance of less than 4 kilometres, and, lacking artillery support and badly exposed in open country, suffered 1,000 casualties. By 19 June the attack had petered out, with the northern and southern thrusts having been unable to meet. Huesca remained in Nationalist hands throughout the war and Franco was not distracted from Bilbao, which fell the same day. The Internationals had been defeated at both Segovia and Huesca not by a colonial elite but by local regular army units. Clearly, offensive operations were still beyond the capabilities of the People's Army.

In order to buy the Northern Zone time, what was required was not limited operations with a handful of divisions but a full-scale offensive. The People's Army attempted its first such assault in July 1937 in the same sector as the Corunna Road battle of the previous winter. Devised and planned by the new Chief of the General Staff Colonel Vicente Rojo, the

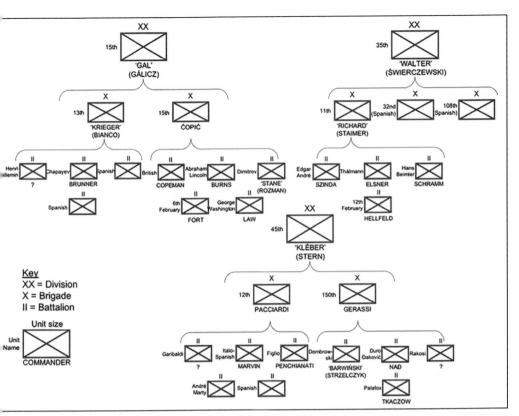

Figure 7. International units at the battle of Brunete, July 1937.

mastermind of the defence of Madrid, the objective was to relieve the siege of the capital by driving two whole corps (totalling six divisions) south from El Escorial to Navalcarnero and the Romanillos heights. Holding these positions would render untenable the Nationalist lines in University City and the Casa de Campo. An additional corps would attack west from positions south of Madrid with the aim of linking up with the main drive, thereby surrounding the Rebel troops on the outskirts of the city. The People's Army was at the apogee of its strength, with 132 tanks, over 140 aircraft, 130 artillery pieces and around 60,000 troops gathered for the attack, many of them veterans of the bitter winter battles. Five International Brigades would take part: the 11th Thälmann (without the Commune de Paris battalion, which had been transferred to the 14th Brigade, but with the addition of a new Austrian unit, the 12th February battalion, making the 11th Brigade a German-speaking unit) was part of General Walter's 35th Division, the reserve of the elite V Corps, commanded by the most talented of the Communist militiamen, the 30-year-old Lieutenant Colonel Juan Modesto. In XVIII Corps, to Modesto's left, was the 15th Division under General Gal, containing the 13th Brigade (French, Belgian and Polish volunteers) as well as the 15th, which had

Italian volunteers of the Garibaldi battalion, 12th Brigade. Although they had fought well at Madrid and Jarama, the performance of the Garibaldis would decline markedly in mid-1937 at Huesca and Belchite.

remained in its positions at Jarama since February. Finally, Kléber's 45th Division (the 12th and 150th International Brigades) had been transferred down from Huesca and would serve as a reserve. This was the greatest assault force the Republic was ever to assemble, particularly in terms of quality of manpower and equipment. The results would be disappointing in what was subsequently to be known as the Battle of Brunete, which would prove to be something of a Somme experience for the new army.

On the night of 5/6 July V Corps, led by Líster's fine 11th Division, infiltrated Rebel lines and advanced through open country to the town of Brunete, which they assaulted at dawn, seizing it quickly. An advance on Navalcarnero was delayed by failures elsewhere which left the Lísters' flanks exposed. The 46th Division to their right failed to take the fortified town of Quijorna in multiple frontal attacks until 9 July, requiring the commitment of the Thälmanns to support the final encirclement and capture of the strongpoint. To the east, on XVIII Corps' front, Villanueva del Pardillo

The Battle of Brunete, July 1937. (*Adapted from Hurtado, 2013. CC BY-SA 3.0*)

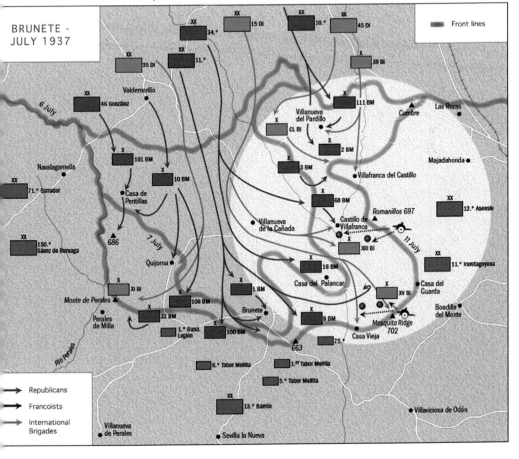

Internationals using a Degtyarev DP-28 light machine gun. Supplied by the USSR, the Degtyarev was well known for its distinctive pan-shaped magazine and would see extensive use in the Second World War. (*Tamiment Library and Robert F. Wagner Labor Archive*)

Republican troops, likely of the 46th Division, advance during the battle of Brunete, directed by 'El Campesino', a famous, if incompetent, militia commander, seen here on horseback. (*reproduced from Book of the XV Brigade*)

A German instructor trains Spanish Nationalists in the use of the Pak 36 AT gun, 300 of which were sold to Franco by Nazi Germany. This weapon proved highly effective at stopping T-26s during the Brunete campaign and as a result Soviet observers would demand thicker armour in the design of their subsequent tank, the T-34. (*Bundesarchiv*)

and Villanueva de la Cañada held up the 10th and 34th Divisions respectively. Already on 6 July Republican command felt it necessary to divert the 15th Division with its two International Brigades from its objective of the Romanillos heights (which scouts reported to be undefended) to Villanueva de la Cañada. Anti-tank and field guns firing over open sights had driven back the Soviet tanks and the Internationals had to advance in the open against machine guns and snipers. Popular British volunteer John Henderson remembered the attack:

> We got to about a quarter of a mile away in a field above the village so that we could fire down on the church [where there were snipers]. Then the order came to attack so we got up but had to keep dropping down again, we didn't get very far before there was fairly intense fire, we had to keep getting up, moving, dropping down to take cover. And then my face was filled with grit. Next thing I knew, I was being dragged back because what had filled my face with grit was a bullet which had landed in front of me and gone through my arm. So I didn't get to Brunete.[21]

As a result, they could not storm the town until the night of 6/7th, when the British, American and Balkan volunteers overwhelmed the defenders. By the time the 13th and 15th Brigades reached their true objective, the important heights overlooking the roads into Madrid, Nationalist reinforcements had been rushed in to defend them. In a series of fruitless assaults, the Internationals suffered huge losses, with the new George Washington battalion being merged with the Abraham Lincoln on 11 July, both units having suffered 50 per cent casualties. The losses included Oliver Law, the Washingtons' commander and the first African-American to lead white troops in combat. With progress slowing, Kléber's 45th Division was thrown in to aid XVIII Corps. The 12th Garibaldi Brigade fought well, storming Villanueva del Pardillo on the night of 10/11 July but then failed to make any headway in the northern portion of the Romanillos heights, falling short of their next objective, Villafranca del Castillo. The 150th Brigade put in a poor showing, its Dombrowski and Palafox battalions assaulting Mocha Hill, west of Villafranca, multiple times from 10 July onwards but, like their British and American comrades further south, failing to make headway while suffering heavy losses. Kléber wrote:

> In front of [Mocha] hill and the barbed-wire obstacles of the enemy was a deep ravine with steep banks. Our tanks got to the ravine and could not move any farther forward. At that point, the enemy anti-

Villanueva de la Cañada, the village stormed by the 15th International Brigade on the night of 6/7 July 1937. (*reproduced from Book of the XV Brigade*)

tank cannon were firing well aimed shots. My infantry got into the barbed wire of the enemy and could not move any farther forward ...

The command staff ... ordered a repeat of the attack on Mocha, in which all the commanders were ordered to go in front of their battalions and lead the men in a bayonet attack.[22]

The attack failed, with many officers lost. Republican high command had, it appears, desperately tried to make up for the opportunities missed in the battle's first day by repeatedly throwing their troops forward until mid-July, despite hardening resistance, heavy losses and the great difficulties brought about by the heat and enemy air power on what was, for the most part, a barren, open plain. Franco had acted swiftly, moving troops and planes down from the north to halt the Loyalist advance and prepare a counter-attack. The Nazi Condor Legion and Italian Legionary Air Force, now powerful forces with hundreds of aircraft, well trained pilots and the latest technology, including the new Messerschmitt Bf-109, were able to sweep the Republicans from the skies and subject the few roads in the sector to constant harassment. Food, water and ammunition

A Messerschmitt Bf-109 of the Nazi Condor Legion in Spain. The famous 109 saw its first combat in the spring of 1937 and at Brunete decisively turned the tide of air superiority in the Nationalists' favour. Franco's air force, dominated by Italian and German planes and pilots, was to maintain control of the skies for the rest of the war.

A T-26 passes through Villanueva de la Cañada during the People's Army's ill-fated advance. (*reproduced from Book of the XV Brigade*)

could only be brought up at night, and the exhausted People's Army could advance no further.

With some of the finest troops in the Rebel army, including Foreign Legionnaires, *Regulares* and two brigades of the fanatical Navarrese Carlists, as well as overwhelming air and artillery firepower, General Varela was tasked with launching the Nationalist counter-attack. From 18 to 23 July they pounded Republican positions but were able to gain just a few kilometres. For the most part the Loyalists held firm in a horrendous battle of attrition. A member of the 15th Brigade's anti-tank battery remembered firing shells directly into clumps of advancing Rebel troops, tearing dozens of them limb from limb. However, having fought for nearly three weeks without relief, the Republicans were bound to break somewhere under the unrelenting pressure. On 24 July a frontal assault by a Navarrese brigade, three Tabors of Moroccans and a Bandera of the Foreign Legion finally broke Líster's 11th Division in the Republican centre, provoking a general retreat. Generals Walter and Kléber were able

15th International Brigade (possibly British) machine-gunners in action during the Brunete campaign. (*reproduced from Book of the XV Brigade*)

to use their Internationals to arrest the rout along a line from Quijorna to Villanueva de la Cañada, although hundreds of panicking men may well have been shot in the process. Meanwhile, orders to withdraw never reached the 15th Brigade, stationed on the south-eastern corner of the Republican salient. The British and 6th February battalions had to carry out a fighting retreat through Rebel lines that reduced both units to company strength. A disproportionately high ratio of the junior officers and commissars who had held the Brigades together in the tough winter battles were among the dead and wounded. Brunete was lost, although the other villages that had been bought so dearly were held. The People's Army had suffered 18,600 casualties (compared to 14,300 Nationalists), but the Republic's loss of irreplaceable experienced men, a third of their tanks and up to a hundred aircraft would have grave implications for the remainder of the war, especially as from the summer of 1937 Soviet shipments began to dry up.

By the end of July the International Brigades were in poor condition. Of the 13,393 foreign volunteers in Spain, the International Brigades had lost at Brunete 779 killed, 2,329 wounded and 392 disappeared (presumably

Yugoslav troops of the 150th International Brigade escorting Nationalist prisoners during the battle of Brunete. The soldier in the foreground appears to be carrying a Chauchat machine rifle.

the majority either captured or deserting). The men had fought bravely, taking well defended villages where Spanish troops had failed, although they were for the most part garrisoned with mere militia and conscripts. As the momentum of the offensive had waned, casualties had mounted for ever-diminishing returns. Even so, the International units held their own against Franco's elite during the counter-offensive. But many were now unhappy at the huge sacrifices being made and were disillusioned by the Brunete defeat. Morale and discipline became a serious problem in the Brigades and several worrying reports were dispatched to Moscow on the state of the troops. Two Brigades were dissolved, the 13th and 150th, owing to a combination of extremely heavy losses, ill-discipline and, in the case of the 13th, mutiny. As usual, the cause of resentment was military rather than political; for instance, the Chapeyev battalion of the 13th Brigade had suffered 75 per cent casualties at Brunete. The loss of their commander, Swiss Communist Otto Brunner, who was severely wounded, likely did not help matters. The French and Belgians of the 13th Brigade were transferred to Dumont's 14th Brigade, which had not been involved in the battle. The veteran Dombrowski battalion formed the core, combined with various Central and Eastern European volunteers from both brigades, for a reconstituted 13th International Brigade of Slavic nationals; it came to be known as the Dombrowski Brigade and regained

(Opposite) Advancing across open plains at the height of summer, Republican forces at the battle of Brunete found themselves exposed both to the intense heat and to Nationalist air power. (*Tamiment Library and Robert F. Wagner Labor Archive*)

a good combat reputation. Leaders of the British battalion were sent home amidst political disputes, and Pacciardi left Spain in similar circumstances, leaving an inadequate commander in the Communist Carlo Penchianti at the head of the 12th Garibaldi Brigade. Thousands of demoralised troops (some wounded, some deserters) flooded the base at Albacete, with many ending up spending time in the re-education camp before being returned to the front. It is worth quoting at some length a confidential report sent to Moscow at this time by a French Comintern representative:

> 11th Brigade: Currently, the international troops of this brigade only account for 10 to 15 per cent of its total troop strength. Until now, because of the high political quality of the soldiers, most of whom are German, alarming signs of disintegration and demoralization have not appeared, but it is worth noting that given the composition of this brigade (15 per cent international and 85 per cent Spanish), the consequences of possible demoralization among the 15 per cent international (German) cadres could be more serious here than anywhere else.

Otto Brunner, Swiss Communist and commander of the multi-national Chapayev battalion that was all but wiped out at Brunete. The 13th Brigade, of which it was a part, mutinied and was dissolved and reconstituted as an exclusively Slavic formation. Brunner himself was severely wounded in the battle.

12th Brigade: The commander of this brigade has recently submitted his resignation [Pacciardi]. This is a very clear sign that the brigade's morale is suffering. Increasing numbers openly espouse the idea that the 400 Italian comrades who remain have accomplished their task, and that the time has come to demobilize them, if the officer corps is not to be decimated by Italian emigration.

13th Brigade: For reasons I have already discussed above, out of combat at present, and undergoing a very difficult reorganization and reconstitution.

14th Brigade: Its commanding officer suspended [Dumont]. Without hope of receiving reinforcements and being returned to normal strength. The brigade's morale is in a worrisome state. In any case, as long as it is not reinforced with troops and arms, it cannot be considered a brigade, because its troop strength is smaller than that of two normal battalions.

15th Brigade: Has withstood enormous losses. Four of its battalions have been consolidated two by two, to form only two battalions. The English battalion has fallen victim to a wave of collective desertions, which has begun to affect the American battalions. The officers are not excluded from this process of demoralization.[23]

Perhaps what is most remarkable is that the International Brigades still existed at all at this point, given that every brigade, save the 11th, appears to have been in extremely poor shape. Truth be told, after virtually non-stop combat since the winter, the volunteers were badly in need of a rest, if not repatriation, especially given the near-uninterrupted chain of military setbacks the Republic had endured, surely wearing down morale and motivation. In an effort to reduce national tensions, the Brigades were reorganised in an effort to make them more linguistically homogenous: the 11th was now solely Germanic, the 12th Italo-Spanish, plus the Frenchmen of the Marty battalion, the reconstituted 13th Slavic, the 14th French-Belgian and the 15th Anglophone, with the exception of the Balkan Dimitrov battalion, soon to be transferred. It goes without saying, however, that each brigade was also, to varying degrees, manned by Spaniards, with each national battalion being complemented by a Spanish company and most International Brigades also having at least one all-Spanish battalion. The heavy losses of the last nine months could not be replaced with new arrivals from abroad. While the flow of volunteers had averaged nearly 3,500 per month up to March 1937, from April to July the average was just

1,500 (and this figure includes wounded men returned to action). Yet somehow the officers and commissars were able to forge the battered remnants and the trickle of new arrivals into crack units once again. The Comintern report quoted above ends on a remarkably upbeat note:

> The picture of the International Brigades' military and political situation sketched here is not as dark as one might think. Doubtless, these processes of demoralization can be stopped. In some cases, the symptoms indicate potential demoralization, rather than the disease itself ...
>
> Now, I believe I can affirm that whatever some say their faults may be, the *International Brigades still represent a quarter of the Spanish army's shock units* [author's italics]. There is not an army in the world that can spare a quarter of its shock units.[24]

Most mixed brigades in the People's Army were inexperienced, poorly trained and equipped, and stocked with conscripts who had not enlisted with either side at the outbreak of civil war and who displayed questionable commitment in both attack and defence. Although many of these defects applied to the Internationals, they were at least ideologically committed to the Republican cause and could be relied upon to fight hard in even the most trying of circumstances. Those International Brigades that remained in decent shape would continue to be Loyalist commanders' most trusted assets.

The Aragon Front

Despite the failure to relieve the siege of Madrid, the Brunete battle had distracted Franco from his northern campaign and delayed his push on Santander for some five weeks. The People's Army had bought a breathing space for their comrades but at an exorbitant cost, as we have seen. By mid-August the beleaguered Northern Zone was in need of assistance once more. Chief of the General Staff Vicente Rojo planned a new offensive on the previously quiet Aragon front, aimed at surrounding and capturing the regional capital Saragossa. Aragon was an appealing theatre for the Republican government not just for military reasons (300 kilometres of frontage was held by just 20,000 Nationalist troops, mainly consisting of conscripts and integrated rightist militia) but they also sought to gain politically. The region was run by the Anarchist Council of Aragon, a revolutionary body set up the previous summer, which had overseen large-scale collectivisation of agriculture. The central government wished

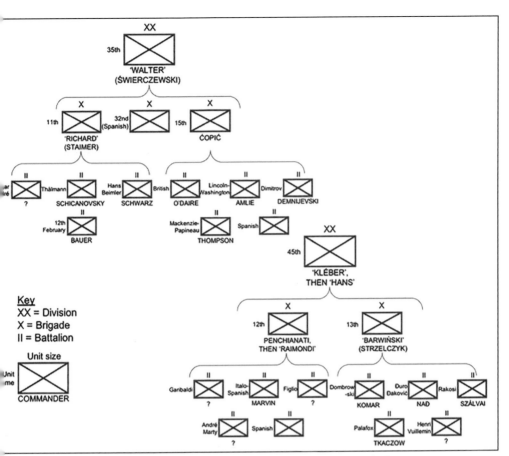

Figure 8. International units at the Aragon offensive, August–October 1937.

to reassert its authority and normalise the economy here, and what better way than to bring the strongest units of the People's Army into the region. The breaking-up of the collectives and the Council completed Prime Minister Juan Negrín's counter-revolutionary programme and was undertaken, not without violence, by the Líster division from 11 August.

By the 24th the Republicans were ready to return to the offensive. Three main drives were launched on Saragossa, with International troops taking part in two of them. North of the river Ebro, one push by Catalan troops of the Karl Marx Division soon became bogged down at the village of Zuera. In September they would be forced back to their start lines by a counter-attack from Mussolini's CTV. Further south, astride the Barcelona–Saragossa highway, General Kléber's 45th Division (including the 12th and 13th International Brigades) attempted to storm the fortified Sierra de Alcubierre without armoured, air or artillery support. The attack began in darkness, but when the sun rose it became apparent that the 12th Brigade's Garibaldi and André Marty battalions had strayed to the right and were

Enemy: Nationalist militia

Just as tens of thousands of Spaniards had joined worker and peasant militias formed by left-wing parties and unions at the outbreak of the civil war, so rightists had flocked to ad hoc paramilitary units created to support the military Rebels. The Falange, Spain's fascist party, saw a surge in popularity immediately before and after the outbreak of war. Their 'Blue Shirts' were the foundation of a militia that would gain a reputation for committing atrocities behind the lines while lacking courage at the front. In fact, Falange units actually fought with great determination in defensive battles at Brunete and Belchite but they were not trusted by Nationalist commanders for offensive operations.

The Carlist Traditional Communion, a reactionary, ultra-conservative monarchist movement, was particularly strong in rural Navarre, in northern Spain. The Carlist militia, known as the *Requetés*, were famous for their red berets and white shirts, as well as their suicidal bravery in combat. Passionately Catholic, the Carlists sought a return to the confessional Spain of the sixteenth century and rejected modernity in all its forms, including, it appears, the concept of military camouflage. Nevertheless, the 1st through 5th Navarrese brigades were the backbone of Franco's northern campaign, and the later divisions into

A Falange rally.

Carlist *Requetés* wearing their distinctive red berets. (*reproduced from Cardozo, 1937*)

which they were expanded were some of the Insurgents' most reliable troops. In April 1937 the Falange and Carlist movements were forcibly co-opted by Franco in consolidating his political hold on the Nationalist zone and formed the basis of the single party, the *Movimentio*, which was to govern Spain until 1975. What independence the militia units had enjoyed from the Spanish military was therefore lost by mid-1937 and they were integrated into army divisions, although the wearing of elements of party uniform, especially the Carlist red beret, remained ubiquitous and units retained their Falangist or *Requeté* identity.

caught in the open below one of the fortified hills. They were pinned down by machine-gun and mortar fire for two days before they were eventually able to retire. The 12th was unable to play a further role in the battle, having suffered 250 casualties. General Walter labelled the Brigade 'unbattleworthy and half-demoralized'. Kléber accused the 12th's new commander, Carlo Penchienati, of deliberately disobeying orders regarding the axis of advance and subsequently spreading lies about his conduct of the attack. Both men would soon be dismissed. The newly Slavic

Balkan commanders: Franc Rozman, known as 'Stane' in Spain, the commander of the Dimitrovs, and Dušan Kveder, a captain in the Slavic 129th International Brigade. Both would become partisan leaders in occupied Yugoslavia in the Second World War, Rozman rising to the rank of general.

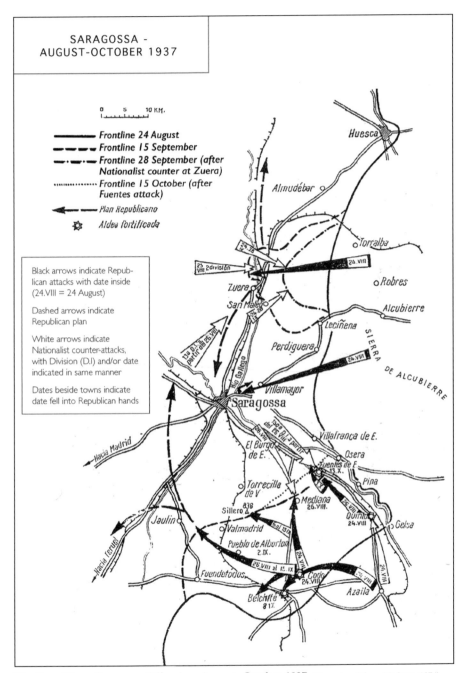

The Republican Saragossa Offensive, August–October 1937. (*Reproduced from Modesto, 1974*)

13th International Brigade performed better, seizing several hill-tops under the cover of darkness on the battle's first morning and then subsequently pushing on to the village of Villamayor de Gallego the following night. This was the closest any Republican forces would get to the ultimate objective of Saragossa during the battle. However, with Kléber unable to send reinforcements to the Eastern Europeans (the 12th Brigade was still pinned down at this point), they were driven out of Villamayor and retreated in disorder:

> The Polish battalions met them [the Nationalists] in a friendly manner, with machine-gun fire. The battle in Villamayor de Galero [*sic*] continued until 1700 hours, when the enemy, advancing with tanks, forced the Poles from the town. They were already running out of ammunition. At dawn the next day, the Polish battalions, reduced to 60 per cent, began to arrive at our deployment area in groups, carrying with them their wounded and four dozen prisoners. The other captured officers had been shot by them when the prisoners refused to go with them and tried to escape under the cover of night. Separated groups of soldiers made it back through the enemy lines for four or five days more.[25]

Colonial troops of the Nationalist 13th Black Hand Division soon arrived in the sector and attacked the 45th's gains repeatedly, with both sides suffering heavily in a series of back-and-forth battles for the key heights. In one such assault the commanding officers of the 4th Bandera of the Foreign Legion and a Tabor of *Regulares* were wounded within moments of going over the top; Kléber's account speaks of piles of dead Moroccans building up on the hillsides. By the end of the battle the Dombrowski Brigade had suffered 800 casualties and was left with just two hill-tops in their possession. Although a capable commander who was probably hard done by in being sacked (and later imprisoned in Stalin's Great Purges), it is hardly surprising that Kléber's political enemies were able to engineer his replacement with Colonel Hans Kahle in September 1937 following the lacklustre performance of the 45th Division at Saragossa.

Simultaneously, on the southern bank of the river Ebro, Lieutenant Colonel Juan Modesto's V Corps, including the 11th and 15th International Brigades of General Walter's 35th Division, pushed up the Quinto–Fuentes–Saragossa road. While Líster's 11th Division made the furthest advance, reaching Fuentes de Ebro on the battle's first day, the 35th was tasked with storming the village of Quinto. Having hoped to secure their

The church at Quinto was turned into a fortress by the Rebel garrison and proved a tough nut to crack. *(Tamiment Library and Robert F. Wagner Labor Archive)*

objective swiftly, it transpired that the village was well fortified and garrisoned by several thousand Nationalist troops, mostly Falange and Carlist militia units, mixed in with conscripts. Loyalist troops pushed into the town on the afternoon of 24 August, supported by a handful of tanks and artillery pieces, plus a small air raid, but were met with fierce resistance, each building having to be cleared with hand grenades, bayonets and improvised nitro-glycerine bombs. The centres of resistance proved to be the imposing church, whose tower was a perfect vantage point for snipers, and Purburrel Hill, a conical-shaped height just south of the town which dominated the flat approaches. On 25 August the British battalion was tasked with storming the hill, on which 500 Rebel troops were well entrenched with barbed wire and concrete pill-boxes. As the British charged up Purburrel unsupported, they came under murderous fire. The battalion commander Peter Daly was killed almost immediately, and his friend and adjutant Captain Paddy O'Daire, formerly of the IRA and Irish Free State army, took command and was to save many British and Irish lives that day. O'Daire coolly refused the orders of his superior, Lieutenant Colonel Ćopić, to press on with the suicidal attack, keeping his men hunkered down on the exposed hillside until nightfall, when they could withdraw safely.

The following morning the British, this time with close fire support from the 15th Brigade's anti-tank battery, was able to storm the hill. For

Nationalist prisoners from the Quinto garrison trooping past Purburral Hill. An unknown number were executed by 35th Division men. (*reproduced from Book of XV Brigade*)

hours the Soviet 45mm guns pounded the Nationalist trenches incessantly, before O'Daire's men finally rushed the position, capturing scores of prisoners.

> Our artillery, especially the anti-tank guns – gave them hell. The little shells went in one continuous scream over our heads and smashed the machine-gun nests. I believe the whole battle lasted five hours. But, that day, I had no sense of time, and my memory of the sequence of events is faulty.
>
> I remember seeing barbed wire ahead, and the brown earth of parapets. I remember Paddy O'Daire's yell: 'Charge the trench!' As we ran up the last few yards, the trench became alive. A mass of white faces, hands upstretched [*sic*] to the sky.[26]

Nevertheless the attack cost many lives, and, without a source of water, it would have been only a matter of time before Purburrel's defenders had to surrender. Within the town itself, 26 August was also the key day as the Balkan volunteers of the Dimitrov battalion stormed the church in scenes reminiscent of a medieval siege (the door was battered down before burning hay bales were tossed inside). The battle for Quinto had taken 48 hours longer than planned and cost the Internationals over 300 casualties. Nevertheless, it had been a clear victory for the 15th Brigade and probably their best executed operation to date, with a US military attaché writing,

> The Chief of Staff of the XV Brigade [Merriman] informed me that the Quinto campaign was well organized and coordinated and that it

was by far the best conducted offensive in which the brigade had participated. In fact, he added, it is the only one where there prevailed combined movement controlled by a central authority in the field with a definite purpose and fixed objectives.[27]

This report implies that the transfer of the 15th Brigade to General Walter's command (having previously served in the reviled General Gal's 15th Division) marked a significant improvement in command and control, and Walter was said by journalists to have an 'exceptionally good' record, and be an expert in offensive operations according to Modesto's memoirs. The 15th Brigade had come a long way from its heroic but incompetent debut at Jarama and was finally living up to the shock troop reputation of the Internationals, albeit at a time when the older Brigades such as the 12th were on the wane. However, the victory brought with it one of the volunteers' darkest moments. Dozens of prisons from the Quinto garrison were shot by the Germanic and English-speaking volunteers of the 11th and 15th Brigades. The 35th Division commander General Walter executed at least one, by some accounts several, Nationalist officers in revenge for the death of a friend, a Polish doctor who headed the division's medical unit. The 15th Brigade's American chief of staff Robert Merriman was said to be dismayed by the violence unleashed by his men and the ill-discipline it engendered. This is the only case known to the author of a major war crime being committed by the International

Nationalist concrete fortifications covering the road into Quinto.
(*Tamiment Library and Robert F. Wagner Labor Archive*)

Brigades, although the shooting of prisoners, particularly officers, in the midst of combat was fairly commonplace on both sides in the civil war and some volunteer accounts do include references to off-hand killings such as these, especially during advances.

Further south, the fortress town of Belchite had been surrounded by Catalan troops but was well defended with numerous artillery pieces and several hardpoints (including two churches), and garrisoned by more than 2,000 Nationalist troops and civilian volunteers, including the town's Falangist mayor, who radioed to Francoist command 'If before you arrive, death arrives, we welcome it! We will resist until we die. Long live Spain! Long live the Army!' Many volunteers would attest to the great bravery and determination shown by the beleaguered garrison, which was resupplied from the air by Franco. While the majority of Modesto's V Corps, including the British battalion, the Lísters and the 46th Division, was busy containing repeated counter-attacks and relief attempts by colonial troops of the Rebel 13th and 150th Divisions (under the experienced generals Barrón and Sáenz de Buruaga), the 15th International Brigade was tasked

The defences of Purburrel Hill, which were overcome by the British battalion, at high cost, only after support fire from the AT guns was brought in.
(*Tamiment Library and Robert F. Wagner Labor Archive*)

Belchite today. The old town was deliberately left in ruins by Franco as a monument to the civil war, although a new town was built a short distance away. (*Shutterstock, Pedrosala 40324780*)

with clearing the town. While the decision to focus on Belchite, rather than pushing on to Saragossa has been criticised, it is likely Modesto realised that the drive on the Aragonese capital had already failed thanks to the arrival of Nationalist reinforcements and he did not wish to repeat the mistakes of Brunete. Therefore the majority of Loyalist strength was concentrated on meeting the Rebel counter-attack, while the 15th Brigade was left to mop up Belchite and win a propaganda coup (the Francoists had been broadcasting that the garrison would be relieved). The Dimitrov and Lincoln-Washington battalions approached the town from the north and north-east respectively on 1 September, but it was not long before progress stalled. The final 450 metres of the approach to Belchite's first buildings was made up of open farmland where the only cover was olive groves and irrigation ditches. Although the Lincolns managed to push up to 200 metres from the outskirts of the town, here they became pinned down by machine guns with interlocking fields of fire and snipers firing from every window, with no further cover to aid the advance. In particular, the large San Agustín church and convent (often mistakenly referred to as a cathedral) dominated the eastern approaches and its belfry was a sniper's dream. On 2 September, with much of the battalion lying prone in irrigation ditches, unable even to sit up without exposing themselves to

Commander: Bob Merriman

(*Tamiment Library and Robert F. Wagner Labor Archive*)

Robert Hale Merriman taught economics at Berkeley, California, before volunteering to fight in Spain. Born in 1908 into a working-class family, his father had been a lumberjack and Merriman was forced during his studies to work in various jobs, from decorator to janitor, further supplementing his income with $7.50 a month from the Army Reserve Officer Training Corps. In 1935 Merriman, like many economists and academics of the time, travelled to the Soviet Union to study the seemingly miraculous industrialisation that Stalin had achieved while the rest of the world languished in the Depression. While conducting research in Moscow, he heard of the outbreak of the war in Spain and underwent something of a moral crisis over whether he should volunteer. Eventually, in the winter of 1936, he made his way to Spain of his own accord (Merriman was not a member of any political party) and joined the International Brigades. Owing both to his very limited military experience, which was rare among American volunteers, and to his propaganda-friendly apolitical status, Merriman rose higher than any other American in the Brigades. He became a legendary figure in the 15th International Brigade, commanding the Abraham Lincoln battalion in their first action at Jarama, where he was wounded, before overseeing the training of the new Mackenzie-Papineau battalion.

> Merriman was one of those rare men who radiate strength and inspire confidence by their very appearance. He was tall, broad-shouldered … The physical strength of the athlete combined with the reserved manners of the scholar. (Voros, 1961, p. 344.)

Finally, in August 1937 Merriman was promoted to 15th Brigade Chief of Staff and was far more hands-on than the Brigade's commander Vladimir Ćopić, with whom he frequently quarrelled. Ćopić was on leave during the Great Retreats of the spring of 1938 and Merriman commanded the 15th Brigade in his absence. He was killed during a chaotic night-time breakout attempt when the Internationals had been surrounded, although due to the nature of the fighting his death could not be confirmed for many months.

fire, pressure was mounting from above to get the 15th Brigade's assault moving again. General Walter ordered Ćopić to push on, and he in turn tasked his chief of staff Merriman and the 15th's Commissar Steve Nelson with persuading Captain Amlie, the Lincoln battalion commander, to push his men forward in a near-suicidal frontal charge. More than a few harsh words were exchanged, with Merriman finding himself in the unenviable position of enforcing an order similar to that which he had resisted so fervently at Jarama. Yet with the troops trapped in the open, the alternatives were not desirable either, as Nelson later explained:

> We had to go forward yet that seemed like suicide. On the other hand, if we stayed in the trench, we'd be picked off like sitting ducks. And a retreat over bare ground would cost more lives than an attack. Therefore we had to go forward.[28]

Desperately searching for a way out of the catch-22, Nelson found a gully or culvert running along the town's eastern edge. The Dimitrovs had been able to gain a foothold in the northern outskirts of the town and cleared a small, one-storey olive factory just 50 metres from the San Agustín and with access to the culvert. This is where Nelson led a small party of Lincolns and soon the factory was reinforced, with machine guns set up and engaging in duals with the snipers in the church. Close fire support was provided by the anti-tank batteries of the 11th and 15th Brigades (each armed with three of the excellent Soviet 45mm cannon) and a handful of T-26s, although the tanks found street-fighting a challenge and

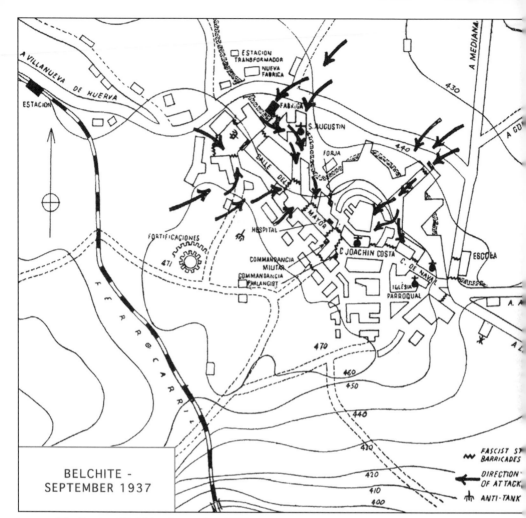

The Battle of Belchite, September 1937. (*Reproduced from The Book of the XV Brigade*)

tended to hang back and bombard buildings from outside the town. The anti-tank weapons in particular proved useful; cooperating closely with the infantry, the gun crews were able to pick off snipers and silence machine-gun nests. The British-manned battery of the 15th Brigade fired no fewer than 2,700 shells from their three guns on the battle's first two days alone. The pivotal day of the siege was 4 September. After two failed attempts to storm the San Agustín, the Lincolns finally unlocked the key to the town's defences. The tanks and anti-tank guns shelled the church intensively, forcing the defenders to take shelter in neighbouring buildings. When the bombardment had finished, three assault parties attempted to rush the church, one led by Merriman running up the gully, one along the road to the church's west and another across from the factory. The attackers moving along the road were caught in deadly machine-gun fire,

The San Agustín Church and convent, often referred to in first-hand accounts as the cathedral. This position was the key to Belchite's defences. (*Wikimedia user Ecelan CC BY 2.5*)

The 15th Brigade's anti-tank battery in action during the Belchite campaign, where their 45mm guns were repeatedly deployed in close support roles, hitting Nationalist hardpoints. (*Tamiment Library and Robert F. Wagner Labor Archive*)

while Merriman was wounded multiple times by grenades, with his face reportedly pouring with blood. A party of Americans managed to get inside the strongpoint just as the Rebels were rushing back in through the main door. A bloody close-range encounter followed but soon the San Agustín was in Loyalist hands and Brigaders began moving into the narrow streets of the town. That night, 15th Brigade staff officer Malcolm Dunbar remembered:

> Belchite presented a picture of the horrors of war which no Hollywood film could ever give. Several large buildings were ablaze. Tongues of flame shot up into the black palls of smoke overhead. The summer breeze wafted across the countryside the stench, nauseating and strong, of dead bodies, human and animal. Above the crackling of the fires maniacal yells arose from some demented creatures whose nerves could no longer stand the strain. Throughout the night the continuous exploding of grenades marked the relentless advance

The olive factory opposite the San Agustín church which was captured by the Dimitrovs and served as the Lincolns' jumping-off point for the assault on the church itself. (*Tamiment Library and Robert F. Wagner Labor Archive*)

of our bombing-squads. It was war shorn of all its glamour, war cruel and bloody – but a war we had to win.[29]

On 5 September bloody house-to-house fighting continued, each building being cleared with grenades and marked as occupied with a red banner. Sometimes charges were used to blast through walls into neighbouring houses. The anti-tank battery was now moved into the streets, firing at the remaining hardpoints of resistance at point-blank range. As evening drew in, the new Brigade commissar, Dave Doran (Nelson had been hit by a sniper and would not see action again) commandeered a propaganda truck with speakers and delivered a clear threat to the last outposts of resistance, now enclosed in a pocket just a few hundred metres across in the south of the town. One Brigader described Doran's speech as 'brief but terrifying in its directness' as he left the garrison with a stark choice: surrender or death. The speech resulted in the surrender of several hundred men, mostly conscripts, convinced the game was up. On the night of 5/6 September what was left of the garrison, along with Nationalist civilians, some 500 all told, staged a number of breakout attempts. One was stopped by the Spanish battalion of the 15th Brigade, with all the Rebel officers killed, possibly executed. A couple of hundred survivors miraculously made it back to Rebel lines. By the morning of the 6th the last resistance was cleared and the town, now nothing more than a wreck of ruined and burning buildings and rotting corpses, was in Republican hands. The prize had cost the 15th Brigade 50 killed and 175 wounded, with a sixth of the Lincolns being casualties, the remainder exhausted. The American Internationals had fought extremely well, although sometimes naively, in their true first experience of urban combat. However, this was matched by the fighting qualities of the Falangist and conscript soldiers of the Nationalist garrison, as the US military mission observed:

> The 'fighting efficiency' of the Rebels based upon their performances at Belchite and Quinto was not only high but well in the category of heroic. Under the most adverse circumstances, they fought, cut off on all sides, to the very last, engaging in hand to hand mêlées and frequently committing suicide as a last resort to prevent capture.[30]

The Saragossa offensive had failed at both operational and strategic levels; not only had the Aragonese capital not been captured, but Franco had not been distracted from his northern campaign by the bitter battle at Belchite, capturing Santander on 26 August before moving on Asturias and the

The narrow streets of Belchite were the scene of some of the bitterest house-to-house fighting of the war. (*Tamiment Library and Robert F. Wagner Labor Archive*)

port of Gijón. With the Republican Army of the North in a state of collapse, the government was desperate to make one last push on Saragossa. On 13 October the 15th Brigade was once again selected to act as shock troops, spearheading an assault on Fuentes de Ebro, which had been on the front line since the first day of the whole operation, when the Lísters had failed to capture it. They were supported by a new formation, the International Tank Regiment, with forty-eight fine BT-5 cruiser tanks from the USSR and volunteer crews fresh from training. The Fuentes attack was also the debut for a new battalion, the Mackenzie-Papineau, made up of

Shock troop leaders – the leaders of the battalions of the 15th Brigade in the Belchite campaign: Robert Thompson of the Mac-Paps (1); the imposing Texan Phil Detro (2), who took over the Lincolns after Hans Amlie was wounded; Paddy O'Daire of the British battalion wearing the baggy officer cap (4); and Captains García (3) and Aguíla (5) of the Brigade's Spanish battalion. (*Tamiment Library and Robert F. Wagner Labor Archive*)

The Mackenzie-Papineau battalion, 15th International Brigade. After several months' training, the battalion's baptism of fire came at Fuentes de Ebro. While nominally a Canadian unit, the majority of its members, including its first commissar and commander, were in fact American.

Tanks of the Spanish Civil War

Even though the Spanish Civil War is often regarded as the opening round of the Second World War, tanks were not a major factor. Just 819 tanks and armoured vehicles of all types were supplied to the Republicans and Nationalists combined over the course of the entire war. To put this in perspective, 552 tanks had been deployed by the Allies alone on 8 August 1918 in the First World War's Battle of Amiens. In comparison, the Republicans never amassed more than around 130 tanks for any one battle. Nevertheless, in the struggle for Madrid of late 1936 and early 1937 the appearance of Soviet T-26 tanks on the battlefield could cause panic in Nationalist ranks, with anti-tank weaponry still lacking on both sides.

The T-26 was a Soviet tank based on the British Vickers 6-tonne design which entered service in 1931. In all, 281 were supplied to the Spanish Republic during the civil war, with the vast majority arriving in the period from the autumn of 1936 to the spring of 1937. During this period the People's Army had a crucial advantage in both quantity and quality of armoured forces. The T-26 was markedly superior to the German Panzer I and Italian CV 33 tankette supplied to the Nationalists, chiefly due to its powerful 45mm anti-tank cannon (the Axis-supplied tanks were armed only with machine guns) and during the battle for Madrid the Soviet and German designs would clash for

The main tanks for the civil war (*from left to right*): T-26, BT-5, Panzer I, CV 33.
(*Contando Estrelas, Flickr, CC BY-SA 2.0*)

the first time, with predictable results. However, their thin armour meant the T-26s suffered high loss rates in the war's major battles and the lessons learnt in Spain would inform the design of the excellent T-34. Initially, the tanks were manned by Soviet crews, although this changed as the war progressed and more Spaniards were trained up. Over the course of the conflict scores of T-26s were captured by the advancing Rebels and put to use in their own armoured units, with some examples remaining in Spanish service into the 1960s.

The Russian BT-5 was the finest tank of the war. It was armed with the same powerful 45mm gun as the T-26 but it was highly manoeuvrable and fast, being capable of speeds close to 50mph. However, the BT-5s did not have a great impact; only fifty were sold to the Republicans, more than a third of which were lost in their first action at Fuentes de Ebro in October 1937.

The Nationalists utilised 122 German Panzer Is, which, like the 155 CV 33 tankettes used by the Italians in Spain, were too lightly armed and armoured to combat other tanks, serving instead in the infantry support role. In their stead, captured Russian machines would prove to be the best tanks in Franco's army, although, like the Republicans, the Nationalists' use of armour was unimaginative, with tanks generally deployed in 'penny packets' for infantry support.

A rare combat photograph from the war: a Nationalist aerial bombardment during the Fuentes attack. (*Tamiment Library and Robert F. Wagner Labor Archive*)

Canadians and Americans, which took the place of the Dimitrovs to make the 15th International Brigade a truly Anglophone unit. However, the assault was an unmitigated disaster; supporting artillery never materialised, troops of the Brigade's Spanish battalion were riding the tanks into battle but were either shot off or fell as battle was joined. The tanks became stuck in the boggy terrain, while the infantry ran into machine-gun fire and barbed wire. Ćopić informed General Walter that the 15th Brigade had lost more killed, wounded and missing in one day at Fuentes than in the six-day assault on Belchite.

The International Brigades were now moved behind the lines to spend their first significant period at rest since November 1936. What state were

A British battalion light machine-gun team in action at Fuentes de Ebro. The battalion commander, Harold Fry, was killed in the attack, the fifth commanding officer the unit had lost in nine months. The constant turnover of junior officers was a major issue for the International Brigades. (*Tamiment Library and Robert F. Wagner Labor Archive*)

the Republic's shock troops now in following the bloody battles of the summer? We have a good idea of the state of the 11th and 15th Brigades of the 35th Division thanks to detailed confidential reports written by their commander General Walter and the American Military Attaché Colonel Stephen O. Fuqua for Moscow and Washington respectively after visits to these units in October, November and December 1937. First, the weapons and equipment of the Brigades. Colonel Fuqua noted that there was no real uniformity in the dress and kit of the 15th Brigade, with 'no evidence of any attention towards cleanliness, care or preservation'. Additionally, the troops' soldierly bearing and appearance 'seemed at a low ebb' with poor parade formations and a lack of training in evidence. Although impressed with the Brigade's 45mm AT gun, Fuqua noted the absence of mortars and the fact that a light field gun would have been more useful to the infantry than the 45mm, especially as AT guns had mainly been used in an infantry support rather than an anti-tank role. Many of the same

Territorial division of Spain in October 1937, after the conclusion of the northern campaign and the relative failure of the Republic's summer offensives. Republican-held territory is dark, Nationalist light. (*Wikimedia User Nordnordwest, CC BY-SA 3.0*)

Disaster: Tank attack at Fuentes de Ebro

One of the blackest days in the history of the 15th International Brigade was 13 October 1937. In theory, the operation at Fuentes de Ebro was a huge opportunity for the Republicans: they had forty-eight brand new BT-5 tanks (the best the war would see), a large concentration in this poor man's war, plus fresh and well trained International troops in the form of the Canadian-American Mackenzie-Papineau battalion. It remains unclear who developed the plan for Loyalist troops to ride the fast cruiser tanks into the Nationalist lines, which was to backfire so spectacularly. The possible guilty parties were the sector commander Colonel Casado, the corps commander Juan Modesto or the 35th Division's General Walter. One volunteer recalled that the plan was Walter's, based on a Soviet propaganda film. The list of flaws with the Fuentes operation is too long to detail in full, but some of the key issues were: a lack of intelligence or knowledge of the ground (the units involved were only brought up to the front on the morning of the attack), a total lack of communication and coordination (the tanks were late, artillery and air bombardment early and some Republican troops, having not been warned of the operation, fired on the arriving BTs), and a poor selection of target and terrain (Fuentes had been under attack for nearly two months and was therefore well fortified, while the assault between the Saragossa road and the banks of the Ebro crossed boggy sugar-cane fields). A paltry air and artillery bombardment went in at 10.00am, but the tanks did not arrive until 1.30pm, roaring across their start lines, the unlucky Spanish troops clinging on for dear life, some falling under the treads. The tankers had driven through the night to the front in order

Knocked out BT-5s in Aragon. (*Bundesarchiv*)

to maintain surprise, but this resulted in the tardy start to the attack and prevented the tankers carrying out any reconnaissance. They were therefore surprised by the muddy terrain, irrigation ditches and an escarpment, all of which slowed or even stopped the tanks and left them vulnerable to artillery and anti-tank fire. A Canadian tanker with the International Tank Regiment described what happened when they reached the Nationalist lines and were hit by a Molotov cocktail:

> The first thing, the motor stopped. The wires burnt ... so we couldn't move. So long as we had ammunition, we kept firing. I gave orders for the driver to get out because the fire began to get closer to the turret.
>
> (Quoted in Petrou, 2008, p. 76.)

As the crew baled out, they were picked off, as were the International Brigade infantry who attempted to catch up with the BTs but came up against determined resistance. The 15th Brigade suffered 46 men killed and 200 wounded, with a further 126 men of the Brigade's Spanish battalion missing after their doomed tank ride. The Mackenzie-Papineaus in their bloody baptism of fire lost 16 dead, 63 wounded and 4 missing. No fewer than nineteen BT-5s were lost, with others damaged, and a third of the International Tank Regiment crews became casualties, all for gains of a few hundred metres.

issues were highlighted by Walter's report on the situation of the International units:

> It is difficult to convey in words the state of [their] weapons and how dirty [they were], especially the rifles. [Walter here is talking of the British and Canadian battalions.] The bores of their barrels were not much different from a seventeenth-century musket barrel found at Belchite. No fewer than 95 per cent of the rifles had no bayonet or cleaning rod, all lost since time immemorial. There was only a handful of cleaning rags in the brigade.[31]

The Polish general wrote of his embarrassment at the fact that a neighbouring Spanish brigade, led by illiterate men promoted from the militias rather than by trained Soviet officers such as himself, appeared more disciplined, soldierly and clean. There were serious administrative problems, discrepancies in the books, and the work of the Albacete base was unsatisfactory, 'every aspect of which needs to be improved'. Table 2 reveals the extent to which the International Brigades were by this time short on International volunteers, and the fact that the Internationals who remained hoarded the leadership positions for themselves at the expense

Lieutenant Colonel Juan Modesto. At 30 years old, Modesto was the leading communist commander in the People's Army. His elite V Corps contained the famous 11th Division and General Walter's 35th Division of the International Brigades.
(Tamiment Library and Robert F. Wagner Labor Archive)

Table 2. Breakdown of fighting strength of the 11th and 15th Brigades
(from Radosh *et al.*, 2001).

	Number	Of whom Internationalists	Percentage of Internationalists
11th International Brigade as of 30 November 1937			
Officers	145	90	62.0%
Commissars	40	20	50.0%
Sergeants	232	96	42.0%
Corporals	221	26	11.8%
Privates	2,263	416	18.4%
Total strength	2,901	648	22.3%
15th International Brigade as of 25 December 1937			
Officers	122	65	54.2%
Commissars	40	23	57.5%
Sergeants	198	143	71.5%
Corporals and privates	2,148	1,081	50.2%
Total strength	2,508	1,312	52.3%

of their Spanish recruits. The 15th Brigade was the exception in that it was the only Brigade still with a majority of Internationalists, even in the rank-and-file. Walter also noted that desertion was a problem at this time, although the point must be made that a clear majority of the deserters were Spaniards rather than Internationals; they had homes and families to desert to, and many were unhappy about being in an International unit, commanded almost exclusively by foreigners who did not speak Spanish and treated them like second-class citizens in their own country. Rumours that captured International Brigaders were routinely shot by the Rebels also contributed to a lack of enthusiasm, as did the 'chauvinism' of the foreign volunteers in believing they were the superior soldiers.

On the other hand, there were clear positives in the reports of both men. During the autumn the International Brigades were officially incorporated into the Republican military (having previously been solely a Comintern concern) and greater discipline and formality were belatedly introduced. Having talked to the men and observed them at mess, at play and in training, Colonel Fuqua concluded their morale and combat effectiveness were strong:

their fighting spirit is evidently high. This can well be understood knowing the soldier types in these International Brigade units – in which they come from the four corners of the earth actuated by those impulses of adventure, wanderlust, hate, political faith which make for the 'to do or die' spirit in men ...

What battle successes these men have attained seemingly have come to them through their strong conviction of the rightness of their cause, of their physical courage, of their personal bravery and through their indomitable spirit to win. Their failures, in most cases, were plainly caused by lack of efficient leadership in the lower grades and almost the total absence of proper field training.[32]

The latter two issues were common throughout the People's Army, which remained desperately short of junior officers and NCOs and severely lacking in serious training, especially any sort of manoeuvres. Even more

Colonel Stephen Fuqua (*right*), American military attaché in Spain, visiting the 15th Brigade with (*from left to right*) Lincoln commander Captain Hans Amlie, Chief of Staff Major Bob Merriman, Mackenzie-Papineau commander Captain Robert Thompson and 15th Brigade Commissar Dave Doran, October 1937. (*Tamiment Library and Robert F. Wagner Labor Archive*)

startlingly, General Walter was impressed by the turnaround in his troops over the winter, having been horrified by their condition in the autumn:

> Much has changed for the better in the brigades of our division [the 35th] over the past few months, after the Saragossa operation. The 11th has become much more exacting, and the 15th sometimes seems completely different from what it was just a short time ago. Both brigades have seriously pulled themselves together and do not intend to rest on their laurels ...
>
> We began with putting our weapons in order, with discipline, shooting practice, and studying of tactics. The 11th Brigade has made a [relatively] good showing and is undoubtedly the best prepared of all the International Brigades. From the start of October up to the moment the division was transferred to Teruel, it worked like clockwork, every day, systematically, tenaciously, and, most important, according to plan. The 15th, because of a number of unfavourable circumstances, began studies a good deal later, but even it has achieved highly appreciable successes, first and foremost in an understanding [of the need for] regular drill every day and for elimination of laxity of discipline. Much still needs to be done ... but today [14 January 1938] it is already possible to confirm that the tide has turned ...
>
> The results can already be seen ... The mood of the fighters and even the wounded is very calm, martial, and, in the opinion of the Spanish command, higher and better than that of any Spanish unit.[33]

While many historians of the Brigades have quoted the issues Walter highlighted, and the fact that, in his eyes, the Internationals compared unfavourably to a neighbouring Spanish unit, they neglect to note these improvements, nor the fact that in the same report the general is clear that well run Spanish formations were the exception rather than the rule: 'Unfortunately, the examples of the 22nd and 96th Brigades can in no way be taken as typical of the entire Spanish Republican Army.' He adds that in the majority of People's Army brigades, the officers are exceptionally callous and show little concern for the welfare of their men, while this was not the case in the International Brigades he commanded, in which the atmosphere was distinctly less formal and more comradely. Therefore, it would be wrong to say Walter considered Spanish units as superior overall to the Internationals and it is revealing – and flies in the face of some of the historiography – to see that Republican high command still valued the International Brigades as high-quality formations. While the golden age of the Brigades was over – there would be no more heroics on the scale of 'saving' Madrid – it cannot be denied that the Internationals were veteran units in which there were still large numbers of highly-motivated officers and men.

In December 1937 the Republicans launched their third major offensive of the war, to encircle and capture the city of Teruel, tucked away in the mountains of southern Aragon. Once again, the primary strategic goal was to distract Franco from his own plans, this time a new attempt to encircle Madrid, scheduled for 19 December. The conquest of the northern zone had freed up 65,000 Nationalist troops and brought the majority of Spain's heavy industry under Rebel control. Not only that, but more than half of the 100,000 prisoners the Francoists took during the eight-month campaign were 'recycled' into the Nationalist ranks, often being posted to quiet fronts or rear area roles, freeing up more reliable troops for offensive

British Labour party leader Clement Attlee visited the Republic and met International Brigaders in December 1937. The British battalion's No. 1 Company was renamed the Major Attlee Company in his honour. Attlee went on to serve as deputy prime minister in Britain's wartime coalition and then as prime minister from 1945 to 1951.

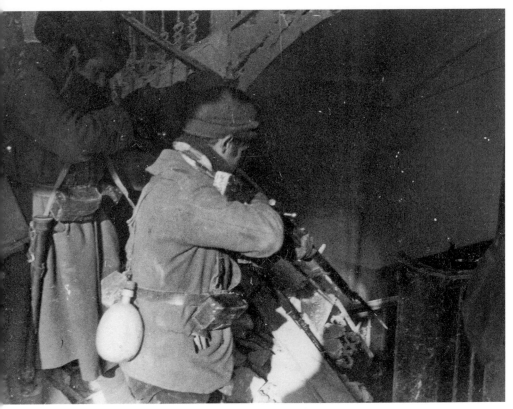

House-to-house fighting in Teruel, initially an all-Spanish operation.

operations. With overwhelming force and firepower poised to assault the 'tomb of fascism', as Republican propaganda had proclaimed the beleaguered capital, Chief of Staff General Rojo designed a plan to throw the Rebels off balance and force them to fight the winter's major battle on less significant ground. On 15 December, amidst bitter snow storms in this, one of the coldest corners of Spain, three corps of the People's Army, led by one of Líster's trademark night infiltration attacks, succeeded in surrounding the city. Next, they cleared the mountain fortresses that overlooked Teruel before moving into the city itself on the 21st. Franco took the bait, shelved his Madrid operation and began to transfer his best units to the Aragon front, although his overwhelming air power was, for the time being, grounded by the atrocious weather conditions, as temperatures plummeted to −20 °C. No International Brigades were involved in the Republican offensive; both for propaganda purposes and to give the battered volunteers a much-needed rest period, it would be an all-Spanish 'show'. However, on 29 December a fierce Rebel counter-attack, under the command of General Varela, began an attempt to relieve the city, where the garrison was still holding out in Stalingrad-esque street fighting. By 31 December Varela's troops, a mixture of Navarrese Carlists and colonial

A T-26 abandoned in the snow around Teruel. Temperatures would drop to record lows of −20 °C during the intense fighting.

A lone Republican soldier advances on the Teruel bull ring.

formations, had broken the Republican lines and were just a few kilometres from Teruel, atop the key height of *La Muela*. At this point Juan Modesto's V Corps was mobilised to breach the gap. The 47th Division retook most of the flat-topped *La Muela*, while the 35th Division took up positions with the 15th Brigade holding a line from the edge of the city running north to the Santa Barbara cemetery hill, and the 11th Brigade to their right, garrisoning another mountain, *El Muletón*. Conditions were testing, with temperatures consistently well below freezing, exposed trenches and problems with getting supplies up to the lines along snow-bound roads. The Lincolns wryly labelled their 'spot' the North Pole, but it was a dangerous part of the line; their latest battalion commander Phil Detro was mortally wounded by a sniper while strolling between positions. The real test came on 17 January 1938 when the Nationalists renewed their drive on Teruel, which had capitulated to the Republicans on 8 January. This time the advance was focused on the Celadas heights, roughly 10 kilometres north of Teruel, and it was carried out by the 13th and 150th Divisions (Foreign Legionaires and *Regulares*) and the 5th Division, a Navarrese unit, with the regulars of the 84th Division supporting the southern flank of the advance. While the colonial troops

International Brigaders on the look-out at Teruel. They display the typical variation in winter uniform. (*Tamiment Library and Robert F. Wagner Labor Archive*)

Lincoln-Washington battalion trenches at Teruel, a spot they labelled 'the North Pole'. Note the Mosin-Nagants' spike bayonet, which many Brigaders found irritating and unwieldy. (*Tamiment Library and Robert F. Wagner Labor Archive*)

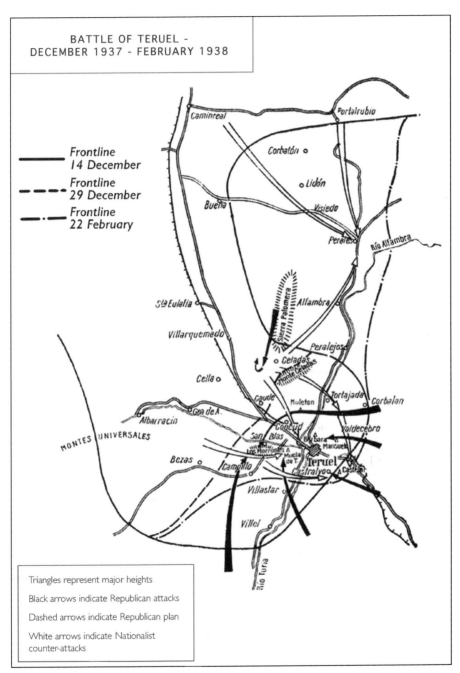

The Battle of Teruel, December 1937–February 1938. (*Reproduced from Modesto, 1974*)

made limited progress in the heights against Loyalist forces, the Red Berets of the 5th Division attempted to storm the 11th Brigade's positions on *El Muletón*. Subjected to murderous artillery and air bombardment, the veteran German and Austrian volunteers of the Thälmann, Edgar André and 12th February battalions held out for three days against overwhelming odds. Lincoln-Washington officer Milton Wolff remembered standing and watching the onslaught grimly as shells fell, dive-bombers swooped down and great columns of Nationalist infantry advanced time and time again. General Walter praised this courageous but costly performance:

> The 11th fought at Teruel ... the most stubborn and powerful battle it had ever had to fight. The brigade behaved heroically, enduring eleven attacks by the enemy over the course of three days at a certain El Muletón. The brigade lost about 1,000 men dead and wounded at the Battle of Teruel [450 wounded, 150 killed, 300 sick]. The battle of Teruel undoubtedly constitutes the most brilliant page in the military performance of the brigade, and the companies of Spanish recruits (Catalan and Madrid) for the first time, showing their very best side, spoke well for themselves.[34]

This is remarkably high praise considering the long history of the 11th and its role in the defence of Madrid. However, once the 11th was forced to withdraw from the hill on 19 January, the 5th Division was able to sweep south down the valley of the Alframbra river, towards the now-exposed flanks of the British and Mackenzie-Papineau battalions of the 15th Brigade. The British battalion was forced to pivot the position of its first company into an exposed line covering the valley, while its machine-gun company occupied an excellent fortified position on Santa Barbara, overlooking both the British and Canadian positions. The Internationals were able to hold the Rebel advance for several days amidst bitter fighting, many insurgents being cut down as they advanced across the open valley and plains, as one green volunteer in the machine-gun company later recalled:

> Suddenly what looked like black ants came crawling up the valley, evidently intent on occupying those forward positions but they had forgotten about us. What a surprise lay in store for them. I for one was almost petrified on looking at hundreds of Fascist troops advancing along the valley, my first view of the enemy. How strange

it all seemed. These black objects, could they be men intent on killing me as well as my comrades? It hardly seemed credible ...

Our heavy gun opened fire and a hail of lead hit the ground a few yards in front of the advancing Fascists, a slight movement of the gun sights and dozens of men collapsed and died. The enemy staggered. At the same time the Canadians on the valley heights opposite opened up with all they had. In a few minutes the valley was completely deserted except for a few score black objects to testify to the enemy's terrible mistake.[35]

Popular Mackenzie-Papineau commander Captain Edward Cecil-Smith, a former sergeant-major in the Canadian army. Reportedly he attempted to desert during the Great Retreats, but he remained the battalion commander until demobilisation.
(*Tamiment Library and Robert F. Wagner Labor Archive*)

By 22 January the Nationalist attack had been halted but both the 11th and 15th Brigades had had a rough time of it. The frozen and exhausted volunteers were pulled out of the line on 3 February.

In an attempt to distract the Rebels from Teruel, the 35th Division was then transferred 80 kilometres north to launch an attack against the village of Segura de los Baños, hoping to penetrate to an important crossroads linking Teruel with Saragossa. On the night of 16/17 February the Mackenzie-Papineaus and Lincoln-Washingtons moved through a snowy ravine in the Sierra Pedigrossa, each tasked with taking a defended hill-top. The Mackenzie-Papineaus reached the base of their objective, Mount Atalaya, without being observed, cut the enemy wire and stormed the hill quickly, taking a hundred prisoners. The Lincolns were slow in getting to their start lines, and the breaking dawn and the firing from Mount Atalaya alerted the second hill-top garrison to the American attack. They stormed it, but at the cost of seven dead. The British and Spanish battalions of the 15th Brigade were tasked with exploiting the gap in the line but failed to make any headway. Two Banderas of the Foreign Legion were

A Maxim-Tokarev machine gun crewed by British gunners in a Teruel trench. The well entrenched machin- gun company proved vital in halting the Nationalist counter-offensive in January 1938. (*Tamiment Library and Robert F. Wagner Labor Archive*)

dispatched by the Nationalists to make an immediate counter-attack on 18 February, and again on the 19th, but these were bloody failures, beaten off first by the British, and then by the 11th Brigade which relieved them. As a German NCO of the Thälmann Brigade took over a British machine-gun nest, he was asked what battalion he was from. The German replied soberly 'Batalión de muerte' (Battalion of the dead). The bloodletting on *El Muletón* had evidently taken its toll. The International efforts at Segura de los Baños were a mere sideshow to the main Teruel battle, however.

A Mackenzie-Papineau battalion man at Segura de los Baños, where the unit fought well. He is using what appears to be a Remington-made First World War era Mosin Nagant rifle. (*Tamiment Library and Robert F. Wagner Labor Archive*)

A Spanish International Brigader dug out of the wreckage after a Nationalist bombardment, Segura de los Baños, February 1938. (*Tamiment Library and Robert F. Wagner Labor Archive*)

On 5 February the Nationalists had launched a new counter-attack further up the Alfambra river, succeeding in just a few days in routing the low-quality conscript formations holding the sector, advancing 20 kilometres and rendering the defence of Teruel untenable. By 19 February Nationalist troops were closing in on the city, and it finally fell to Franco on the 22nd, further advances being halted only by Modesto's organisation of a new defensive line a few kilometres east of the city. Although General Rojo had succeeded in distracting the Rebels from their Madrid plans, his well executed encirclement operation had come to nothing and cost the Republicans dearly. The 60,000 Loyalist casualties (compared to the Nationalists' 57,000) were losses the Republic simply could not afford, especially as much heavy equipment and a significant portion of the air force had been lost in the three-month struggle. The International Brigades involved in the battle had undoubtedly fought well, but their efforts had come to nought. Franco was now poised to deliver the final blow.

Chapter 4

Disintegration, Reformation, Last Stand
March–October 1938

The Great Retreats

Just two days after the conclusion of the Teruel battle, Franco held a conference setting out his planned offensive in Aragon. A huge force, the biggest assembled so far in the war, was to strike eastwards along a broad, 125-kilometre front running south of the river Ebro. From north to south the Nationalists deployed their Moroccan Corps under General Yagüe, consisting of many colonial Army of Africa units, the Italian CTV and the Galician Corps under General Aranda. At Madrid the International Brigades had faced a force of 10,000 Rebel troops. Now, all the brigades would be deployed to try to halt the advance of 160,000 Nationalists, supported by 600 artillery pieces, 350 aircraft and 2,500 cavalry to exploit the open plains over which the advance was to be made. The Republican high command was taken totally by surprise when Franco's Aragon offensive was launched. General Rojo had expected the Nationalists would require at least two months to recover from the losses at Teruel. The operation began on 9 March 1938 and smashed through the weakly held Loyalist lines. The 11th and 15th International Brigades were at rest behind the front, but soon came into action as Yagüe's men achieved a 36-kilometre advance on the opening day, threatening the town of Belchite which had been so fiercely contested the previous year. The Lincoln-Washington and Mackenzie-Papineau battalions fought a short, bloody, house-to-house battle to defend the town but were swiftly forced to abandon the hard-won prize. The 15th Brigade retreated to Lécera but was forced to withdraw again the following day (11 March) as the Nationalist advance continued relentlessly. On 10 March, having arrived from Extremadura, the 12th International Brigade fought to defend Mediana and the lines around Fuentes de Ebro but was soon driven back. The 11th Brigade was

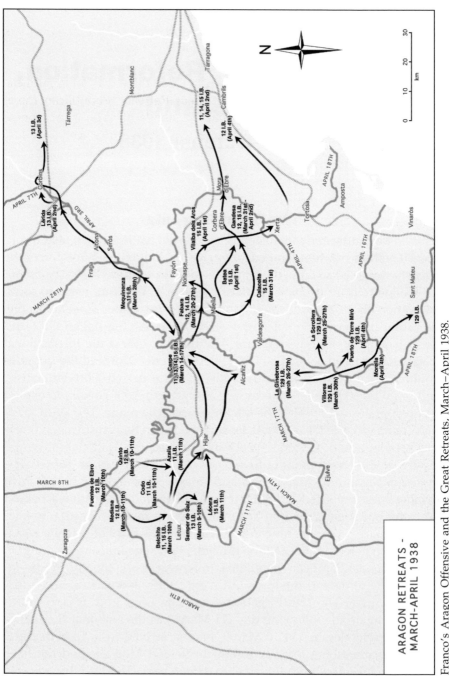

Franco's Aragon Offensive and the Great Retreats, March–April 1938.

forced out of Quinto and Codo on the 10th, then Azaila the following day. All the gains from the Saragossa offensive of August–October 1937 had now been lost. The entire Republican XII Corps, of which the International units were a part, was soon in headlong retreat. The Aragon Front collapsed. In any practical sense, it ceased to exist; there was no Republican line. In what became known as the Great Retreats, Republican forces streamed eastwards, occasionally making stands at various Aragonese and Catalan towns, only to find themselves encircled as units on their flanks fled. Precious equipment, weapons, supplies and military vehicles littered the roads as the Army of the East capitulated. It was a game of cat and mouse as the International battalions, largely operating independently (communication at brigade level and higher was sometimes nigh-on impossible as headquarters moved daily), tried to outrun their Nationalist pursuers, occasionally turning to fight a delaying action.

General Rojo concentrated the fragments of the crumbling front at Caspe in eastern Aragon, where he intended the People's Army to make a stand. After a chaotic fighting retreat through Híjar, the 11th, 12th and 15th Brigades gathered here, alongside the newly arrived 13th and 14th

Dejected-looking Internationals retreat towards Caspe during Franco's Aragon offensive, March 1938. (*Tamiment Library and Robert F. Wagner Labor Archive*)

International Brigades from the Madrid front. One volunteer described the bitter fighting the British battalion engaged in on the edge of the town:

> That night the Battalion alone held the main ridge defending Caspe. The next few days were hectic but the remnants of the Battalion held together. Many hand-to-hand encounters took place. If the enemy had only realised how really few the defenders were, we would have been overwhelmed in a few hours. A couple of hundred Englishmen fought like demons. They literally drove tanks back although only armed with rifles and hand-grenades [these were Italian light CV 33 tankettes, their armour in places just 6mm thick]. One lad from Manchester destroyed two light tanks with machine-gun fire ... A Spanish teniente [lieutenant] ... waited behind the house and watched for the first Italian tank to appear. Sure enough one rumbled cautiously along. As [it] passed the house the teniente flung two well aimed grenades. That tank troubled us no more. Innumerable stories have been told of those desperate days, but once again enemy pressure increased, more tanks were flung in against the thin Republican line and Caspe was abandoned.[36]

Nationalist forces on the march: cavalry and a CV 33 tankette of the CTV advance un-opposed. (*Bundesarchiv*)

After several days of bloody fighting, the town was surrounded on 16 March and surrendered the following day. The shattered remnants of all five Brigades withdrew once again, desperate for respite. In ten days the Nationalists had captured an area of over 7,000 square kilometres and were preparing to advance to the Mediterranean. This was exactly the sort of breakthrough the Republicans had failed to achieve in their own offensives, and owed much to the superior Nationalist logistics and organisation allowing them to exploit breaches in the line far more quickly. It must also be said that the Republic was never able to field such a large force enjoying such levels of firepower for any of their operations as the Nationalists deployed for the Aragon offensive. Meanwhile, the People's Army was in a state of chaos and disintegration, with widespread panic and a collapse in morale. It was widely believed in the ranks that the war was over and that all that remained was to get to safety. While some Internationals also made a run for Barcelona and its port, or else the French border, the vast majority remained. They were depleted and demoralised, but they continued to make stand after stand. Alvah Bessie, a Communist journalist from New York, joined the Lincoln battalion at this stage;

A German Panzer I smashes through a wall during Franco's Aragon offensive, March 1938. (*Bundesarchiv*)

transported with a group of recruits up from Albacete, he described the dejected veterans he encountered:

> Scattered over the side of this wooded hill that commanded a mag-
> nificent view of the mountain scenery near Gandesa and Batea, we
> found a little over a hundred men, disorganized, sitting, lying,
> sprawling on the ground. They had week-old beards; they were filthy
> and lousy; they stank; their clothes were in rags; they had no rifles, no
> blankets, no ammunition, no mess kits, no packsacks. They had
> nothing but the rags in which they were dressed and the filth with
> which they were covered. They were not interested in us. They did
> not greet us; but rather, they looked at us with obvious cynicism.
> They did not speak to us at first; they ignored us; they did not answer
> our questions except in grunts or with expletives ... After we were
> assigned to companies which were hard to find because no one knew
> just where they were, we reported to a ragged man who admitted to
> being in command, and sat down, listening to these men talk.
>
> Here was apparent total demoralization, utter fatigue, rampant
> individualism. The men criticized their command mercilessly; it
> sounded like treason to us.[37]

At Batea the 15th Brigade managed to get a few days' much-needed rest and received reinforcements. There were efforts to reinvigorate flagging morale, some positive – such as exhortations to resist printed in unit newspapers – but others more sinister. One American commissar, Sander Voros, later wrote that his superior, Dave Doran, began a series of courts martial in an attempt to root out cowards and stiffen the unit's fighting spirit. He sentenced a number of volunteers to death for abandoning their posts or deserting during the retreats. However, before any of the con-demned men could be executed, the 15th Brigade's commander, the much-maligned Vladimir Ćopić, returned from leave and ordered, wisely, that the men be given another chance, for the effects of such executions on morale would surely be negative at this delicate moment. Undoubtedly, however, some Internationals were shot as deserters during the chaos that spring. By late March it had become clear that the objective was survival: to reach safety on the north side of the great Ebro river by way of a fighting retreat. The 11th Brigade had crossed on 28 March and held the Rebels at Mequineza. From 20 to 27 March the 12th and 14th Brigades bravely held the Rebels at Fabara but were eventually broken. Further north the 13th Brigade had retreated to Lérida, supporting El Campesino's

Russian BT-5 cruiser tanks of the International Tank Regiment withdrawing during the Great Retreats, Batea, April 1938. (*Tamiment Library and Robert F. Wagner Labor Archive*)

46th Division in its defence of the Catalonian city before it fell on 2 April, and then continued to withdraw northwards. Simultaneously, elements of the rapidly disintegrating 15th International Brigade made a bloody stand at Calaceite on the 31st, and then, with the Nationalists crossing into Catalonia, were forced out of Batea on 1 April. On the morning of the 31st the British battalion had marched out of Calaceite to plug a gap in the line, only to be caught in the open by Italian CTV forces, as a British company commander, Lieutenant Walter Gregory, later remembered:

> What was not known either by Brigade or Battalion staff as we moved forward was that the Lísters [Republican 11th Division] had already retreated even as we approached the front and that we were about to receive the full force of the Fascist advance in that sector. As we turned a bend in the road we ran foul of a column of enemy light tanks which were bound for Calaceite. Another group of tanks broke cover from a wood on our flank and Italian infantry in large numbers entered the fray in support of their armour. All hell broke loose as enemy tanks and infantry poured fire into the leading companies of the Battalion and as soon as the order was given to scatter and make for the hills we broke into ones and twos and sought cover wherever we could find it. Fortunately our Machine-Gun Company, which had been at the rear of the Battalion, was able to secure some high ground

and bring its guns quickly into action, thus affording crucial covering fire while those of us on the road sought to disengage ourselves from the fighting and make good our escape …

So fierce was the fighting that we had no opportunity to gather together our wounded and take them with us …[38]

Gregory gathered together a few dozen men and they made their way back through country crawling with enemy troops to Calaceite, only to

Alvah Bessie, a journalist and later Hollywood screen-writer, served in the Lincoln-Washington battalion. Bessie's account of the war, *Men in Battle*, is frank about the levels of demoralisation during the spring of 1938. (*Tamiment Library and Robert F. Wagner Labor Archive*)

find it already occupied by the Rebels, forcing them to make instead for Gandesa. This débâcle is cited in Hooton's military history of the civil war to demonstrate the regression of the Internationals as military units, for they had advanced with scouts in open formation at Brunete. However, while there is little doubt the Brigades had declined, the comparison is rather unfair, for at Brunete the Republicans were undertaking an offensive, with rested and confident troops expecting to encounter enemy positions, whereas clearly the British at Calaceite simply thought they were marching up to the line and were a shattered unit coming off the back of three weeks of retreat. Brigader Bob Cooney also records in his memoirs that the British had sent scouts out ahead of their column but that they were killed or captured by the Italians. Meanwhile, other troops of the 15th Brigade had withdrawn to the town of Gandesa, further east, and were there joined by the remnants retreating from Calaceite and Batea. Once again the 15th Brigade set out to make a stand at Gandesa, joined by

A forlorn Bob Merriman looks out from 15th Brigade HQ at Batea during the Great Retreats, just days before he was killed among a group of Americans attempting to escape Rebel encirclement. (*Tamiment Library and Robert F. Wagner Labor Archive*)

Enemy: CTV

The *Corpo Truppe Volontaire* (CTV) was a force sent to Spain by Mussolini's Italy to furnish direct military support to Franco's Rebels. At its height it consisted of over 48,000 men, and as many as 78,700 Italian military personnel served in Spain over the duration of the war. The CTV was equipped with some high-quality new weaponry but also much that was substandard or of First World War vintage. The most obvious example was the CV 33 tankette, which was no match for the Loyalist T-26s and in some cases could even be taken out with heavy machine-gun fire. The CTV consisted of one regular motorised infantry

CTV troops retreating during the battle of Guadalajara. (*Bundesarchiv CC BY-SA 3.0 DE*)

division, the Littorio, as well as variously either two or three divisions of Italian fascist Blackshirts (many of them recent recruits from impoverished southern Italy), plus several brigades (which later became two divisions) of Italian army officers and specialists commanding Spanish troops. The CTV's military record was decidedly mixed; in their first action in February 1937 they stormed Malaga, routing militia defenders, yet just a month later at the battle of Guadalajara they were humiliated by the nascent People's Army. Deployed on the northern Front from March to October 1937 they played a key role, and to some extent recovered their ruined reputation, accepting the surrender of the Basque army in August. In Franco's big Aragon and Catalonia offensives of 1938 the CTV once again performed well, albeit putting to flight far inferior opponents. However, once the war was over, the CTV left all their equipment and vehicles in Spain, and the cost of intervention in Spain significantly retarded the Italian war effort in the coming Second World War.

the Garibaldis of the 12th Brigade, but soon the Internationals were totally overwhelmed. After the fall of Gandesa on 2 April the volunteers made a run for the Ebro in disorder. At one point a lost group of Lincolns found themselves literally walking through a Rebel unit's camp as dawn broke, tripping over sleeping Nationalist soldiers. On the night of 2/3 April the Spanish company of the Lincoln-Washington battalion was left defending a hill-top as the American volunteers attempted a night-time dash to the river. On the road north they ran into a Nationalist patrol and chaos ensued, with 15th Brigade Chief of Staff Bob Merriman and Commissar Dave Doran, among many others, disappearing, never to be seen again. During the retreats countless Internationalists fell into Rebel hands, only to be shot out of hand by their captors. One such incident was recorded by Peter Kemp, a rare British volunteer in Franco's elite Foreign Legion, when he was ordered to shoot, in cold blood, an Irish International Brigade deserter captured by his unit.

While some Internationals reached Móra d'Ebre in time for a relatively orderly, if disheartening, crossing amidst streams of Loyalist troops, others, such as the Lincolns' commander Milton Wolff, were forced to swim across the river after spending days behind enemy lines. Further south the new Slavic 129th International Brigade had arrived from Extremadura, fighting its first action on 26 March at La Ginebrosa. Like the rest of the Republican army, the troops of the 129th were soon in full retreat; after losing the fortress town of Morella on 4 April, their subsequent retirement paved the way for the Rebel advance to the sea. Nationalist troops reached

An International Brigader conducting a fighting retreat, April 1938.
(*Tamiment Library and Robert F. Wagner Labor Archive*)

Vinaròs on the Mediterranean coast on 15 April, cutting the Republic into two huge zones, with Catalonia isolated in the north. Defeat was total for the People's Army, which suffered 25,500 casualties up to 1 April, losing over 15,000 small arms and 110 artillery pieces. Nationalist losses to mid-April were a little short of 17,000.

The Battle of the Ebro

After the Aragon retreats, the International Brigades had practically ceased to exist. Some battalions had been wiped out, others numbered just 100 or 200 men. Rumours were rife that the Brigaders were about to be sent home – they had done their bit, they were now militarily useless and the war was surely almost over. Most Internationals probably wanted to leave at this point and they had real hope that a withdrawal was on the cards. The Non-Intervention Committee in London (which upheld the aforementioned Non-Intervention Agreement of 1936) had been discussing a proposal to oversee the withdrawal from the conflict of all foreign volunteers on both sides, an initiative that would ultimately come to nothing due to Franco's stubborn refusal – by this stage the Italian and

German personnel in his forces far outnumbered the International Brigaders. In fact, the Republican leadership was determined to fight on regardless. Defence Minister Indalecio Prieto was sacked for his defeatism and Prime Minister Negrín, who took over the Defence Ministry personally, insisted the People's Army *fortificar* ('dig in'), the new Republican slogan being 'To Resist is to Win'. Behind the scenes Negrín was well aware of the hopelessness of the Republic's position, but his secret approaches to Franco had been met only with demands for unconditional surrender which could not be accepted. The fight had to go on and the International Brigades were not being sent home quite yet.

It was time for the difficult task of reconstruction to begin. The Internationals' base and camps at Albacete had closed down on 19 March and the administration had moved on 2 April to Barcelona in Catalonia, where the volunteers were now cut off. Former Garibaldis commander Carlo Penchienati wrote that there was a real fear, not least from André

Territorial division of Spain in July 1938, after the Great Retreats and Franco's failed drive on Valencia. Republican-held territory is dark, Nationalist light.
(*Wikimedia User Nordnordwest, CC BY-SA 3.0*)

During the long rest period from April to July 1938, various fiestas and competitions were organised, including a football match between the 15th Brigade's British and Spanish members; the Spanish squad is pictured here. (*Tamiment Library and Robert F. Wagner Labor Archive*)

Marty himself, that their train would not make it to Catalonia as the Rebels closed on the Mediterranean coast. This fate did indeed befall the 129th International Brigade, which was stuck in the central zone of the Republic and participated in the halting of the Nationalist drive on Valencia. Despite the establishment of a rallying centre at Cambrils, west of Barcelona, which gathered stragglers and deserters, a considerable number made it across the French frontier or to the safety of the consulates and diplomatic missions in Barcelona. The supply situation in Catalonia was at least tolerable; not only was Barcelona the centre of the Republic's war industry, but the sympathetic French government had temporarily opened the border at the height of the spring crisis, allowing arms shipments from the Soviet Union and Czechoslovakia to re-equip the People's Army divisions marooned in the region, the Mediterranean supply route having been largely cut off by Axis naval forces. This meant that the Brigades were actually at their peak in terms of equipment, at least in terms of small arms, in the coming battle, having received high-quality Czech arms such as the Vz. 24 Mauser rifle and ZB 26 light machine gun. The Red Army and Comintern appointees such as Walter and Ćopić were for the most part recalled, with Kharchenko (the *nom de guerre* of

Ukrainian officer Mikhail Khvatov), the former military adviser to Kléber, the only one remaining in command, leading the Slavic 13th Dombrowski Brigade. In truth, Soviet interest in what they saw as a lost cause in Spain had been on the wane for some time, with few arms shipments arriving between August 1937 and June 1938, exactly when the Republic had most needed their only ally. Italian piracy in the Mediterranean also played a role in cutting off supplies. In place of Moscow's commanders, Spanish officers took over the 35th Division and some International Brigades, such as Major Valledor, the new commander of the 15th Brigade. An Asturian Communist and veteran of the 1934 rising, Valledor had made it back to the Republic after the Northern Zone had fallen to the Rebels the previous October. The German volunteer Hans Kahle was the only foreigner now heading a division in the People's Army. Little wonder that the Internationals were now playing second fiddle; the Brigades were overwhelmingly Spanish in their make-up. Conscripts from Catalonia and elsewhere had filled up the ranks of the decimated battalions, with the Lincoln-Washingtons having just 200 Americans to 500 Spaniards, while the British battalion's 650 men were only a third British. The three International Brigades of the reorganised 35th Division (11th, 13th, 15th Brigades) had a total strength of 11,817, of whom only 30 per cent were foreign, the lowest ratio being in the Dombrowskis at just 15 per cent. The quality of the Spanish troops in the International units was also not what it had been. Although there was a small core of Spanish veterans who had been fighting with the Brigaders for a long time, the majority in each battalion were fresh recruits, with many being either too young to have been called up previously or former deserters, convicts and others who had hitherto been passed over by the draft. Additionally, the International Brigade rearguard was ruthlessly scoured for any remaining Internationals and, alongside the Spanish conscripts, the ranks of the International Brigade battalions were filled with base personnel, support staff, truck drivers, artillerymen and the remaining deserters who had been interred in Brigade labour or re-education camps, which were now closed. These men included known shirkers, those broken by previous combat experience and those volunteers who had previously been considered too old to serve at the front (some were in their fifties). Milton Wolff, the commander of the Lincoln-Washington battalion at this time, admits in his autobiographical novel that a serial deserter who was sent back to the unit was executed in cold blood as it was believed he could not be trusted at the front and would merely be a burden on his comrades. Meanwhile,

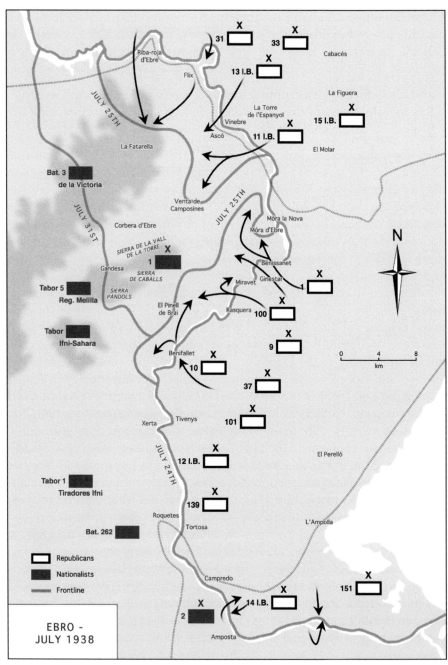

The Republican advance in the Battle of the Ebro, July 1938.

Alvah Bessie painted a vivid picture in his account of the war of the quality of the new Brigaders, both Spanish and International:

> [On the Internationals] New men had come from the auto parks, from soft jobs in Barcelona, from hospitals, from jails and labor battalions, and altogether were a crummy bunch. There was little discipline and less morale. Many of the men were definitely unfit for service, either physically or psychologically ... men who had been in action previously and then transferred behind the lines, but who had been so demoralized by action as to be worthless. You knew they would fuck off if they had the opportunity and the guts – they talked of it continuously. There were a few others who had come for adventure and had found it not quite what they expected; they had deserted, spent some time in jail or labor groups, and were now, in this emergency, sent back ...
>
> [On the Spanish recruits] All were young, between sixteen and twenty; many had never shaved; most were conscripts from farm, factory and office, and had received their little training in Villasecca. Many were from the province of Alicante in the south ... They were ill at ease; they seemed unhappy; certainly few held any convictions about the war and now had left their homes, their parents, for the first time in their lives. To go to war.[39]

Despite all the problems facing the International Brigades, veterans recalled later a real excitement and anticipation at the prospect of a return to action that summer. The Brigades enjoyed perhaps their longest period of rest for the duration of the war as April, May, June and most of July were spent rebuilding, re-equipping and training up the new arrivals in southern Catalonia. Games and fiestas were held to raise morale and keep the men busy. As mentioned above, they were better equipped than previously. Commissars focused on educating the new conscripts about fascism and the causes of the war and, at least according to Bessie, elicited some enthusiasm from the impressionable young men, especially after the deadly bombing of Alicante by the Italians in May. The troops went on manoeuvres and began to practise river crossings. After the pessimism of March and April, there was a new-found optimism when rumours spread that the Republic was in fact to go on to the offensive. In truth, both veterans and new recruits were keen to actually get into combat after months of uncertainty and dress rehearsals, but Brigader memoirs also exhibit a sense of excitement at the chance to make good the losses of the spring and be involved in a bold operation. Writing decades later, they still displayed a sense of pride in being part of the Ebro offensive. Commitment to the Republican cause appeared still to be strong on the whole, although a growing number of volunteers naturally felt it was time to return home. There was one more battle left to fight before their wish came true. Unfortunately, many would not survive this, the longest battle of the war.

The Ebro offensive was launched for two reasons: first, to relieve the pressure on the Levante front as the Nationalists closed on Valencia, and secondly, so that Prime Minister Negrín could prove to both domestic and foreign audiences that the war was not lost and the Republic was still fighting. After his triumphant Aragon advance concluded in April, Franco had defied the advice of his generals and struck south at Valencia rather than north into Catalonia, where, as we have seen, the People's Army units were in a poor state. Instead, he ran into prepared defences, difficult terrain and poor weather as the Rebel army stuttered slowly but inexorably towards Valencia through May, June and July 1938. This

An American volunteer posing with new Czech equipment, in this case the ZB-26 light machine gun, which was copied by the British army to make their famous Bren gun. (*Tamiment Library and Robert F. Wagner Labor Archive*)

By this stage of the war the Brigades were becoming more Spanish – pictured here is Major José Antonio Valledor (*centre*), who was appointed commander of the 15th Brigade after the Great Retreats. (*Tamiment Library and Robert F. Wagner Labor Archive*)

allowed the International Brigades and the other formations of the new Army of the Ebro the breathing space to rebuild. The Republican government's best hope in the conflict remained some form of international intervention; they hoped for foreign mediation, perhaps from the League of Nations, but this was not going to happen if it was widely believed that Franco was on the brink of final victory. Therefore the Ebro operation was designed to prove to the international community that the Republic was still alive and kicking. Certainly, many Loyalist soldiers also hoped it would reunite the divided Republican zones, although it is unclear if this over-ambitious goal was ever General Rojo's intention. Instead, like the operations at Brunete, Belchite and Teruel, Rojo's plan for the Ebro battle was to distract Franco and regain the initiative. Foreign volunteers now made up only 10 per cent of the roughly 70,000 men of the Army of the Ebro, with Spaniards, as we have seen, making up the clear majority even of the International units. Historians have used these figures to make the point that the International Brigades were no longer militarily significant, and indeed, proportionally, there were fewer foreigners in the Republican ranks than at the Battle of Jarama, for instance. However, the fact that

Colonel Modesto, overall commander of the Army of the Ebro, would repeatedly deploy the 35th and 45th Divisions, with their five International Brigades, in the toughest spots in both attack and defence suggests that Loyalist commanders still viewed the Internationals as reliable shock troops. Indeed, given that the Army of the Ebro had been built by combing Catalonia in the spring and early summer of those too old or too young previously to have been conscripted, the small cadre of experienced, battle-hardened Internationalists were, alongside the veterans of the Lísters, the safest pair of hands in an otherwise deeply inexperienced force. While it may be true that 7,000 foreigners in a Republican military that, in total, numbered perhaps 800,000 at this point was a tiny number, the volunteers' relevance is better illuminated by how those 7,000 were used. And at the Ebro they were the tip of the spear.

On the night of 24/25 July 1938 Modesto's army staged a surprise attack across the river Ebro. In defence, the Nationalist 13th, 50th and 105th Divisions of Yagüe's Moroccan Corps were caught completely off guard,

Figure 9. International units at the battle of the Ebro, July–September 1938.

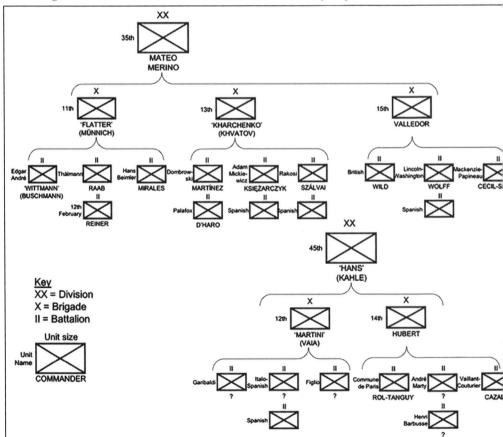

Commander: Juan Modesto

Born in 1906, Juan Modesto was the *nom de guerre* of the Spanish Communist Juan Guilloto León, who served as a commander in the Republican People's Army. Modesto worked at a sawmill in Andalusia before joining the Spanish Foreign Legion and gaining the rank of corporal during service in Morocco. In the 1930s he joined the Spanish Communist party and attended a training course at the Soviet Frunze academy. When civil war broke out, Modesto became one of the leading figures in the Communist militia and displayed great courage and leadership in the war's early battles. The People's Army (formed from the various political militias from autumn 1936 onwards) was desperately short of professional officers and as a result many brigades and even divisions ended up being commanded by unqualified militiamen. Modesto, however, was the outstanding figure of this generation of leaders. Promoted to lieutenant colonel aged just 30 in early 1937, he was placed in command of the Republic's most prestigious unit, V Corps, in which were concentrated the finest Republican troops. At different times various International Brigades served in V Corps, which was frequently used as the People's Army shock formation, with the 11th and 15th International Brigades serving this role in the battles of Belchite and Teruel. Modesto was a ruthless but talented commander, favoured by the Republic's Chief of the General Staff Vicente Rojo for his dependability over the lacklustre Loyalist professional officers and ignorant militiamen. Like other Spaniards who had served in Morocco, Modesto had a tendency to be brutal and caustic, often falling out with other leading commanders, most notably the Communist hero Enrique Líster. He would go on to take supreme command of the Ebro offensive in 1938 and ended the war with the rank of general – an incredible achievement for an uneducated worker-soldier.

Modesto at Brunete. (*reproduced from Modesto, 1969*)

Crossing the Ebro, July 1938. A wave of optimism swept through the People's Army as it took up offensive operations once again. (*Tamiment Library and Robert F. Wagner Labor Archive*)

to the extent that senior staff of the 50th Division were captured in the battle's first morning. The main Republican thrust was carried out by V Corps, under the command of Líster, consisting of the 11th, 45th and 46th Divisions, and XV Corps, under the 25-year-old Manuel Tagüeña (a Communist physics graduate who had been conscripted into the pre-war army), which included the 35th Division. These two corps, with around 60,000 men and 129 guns, quickly punched a hole in the Rebel lines along the northern and southern halves of the great bend in the lower Ebro, their objective being the communications centre of Gandesa and the heights around it, some 25 kilometres from the river. Once this objective had been seized, General Rojo planned an additional phase of the operation involving a motorised drive south-east to Vinaròs and the Mediterranean, although this was never to materialise. The crossing provided a moment of high drama; already in May volunteers of the 13th International Brigade had swum the Ebro to prove the viability of the undertaking. On the moonless night of 24/25 July swimmers stealthily crossed the river to the Nationalist bank and neutralised key defences with grenades. They were soon followed by boatloads of Republican assault troops, while engineers quickly began work on pontoons. In this manner

Pontoon bridges and ferries failed to supply the reinforcements and supplies required to maintain attacking momentum, and many were damaged by Nationalist air raids.

the 13th International Brigade completed a textbook crossing south of Ascó by 2.00am and had secured the town of Venta de Campesinos, some 5 kilometres inland, by 8.00am, capturing a Rebel command post and artillery battery. The 11th International Brigade crossed the river at Ascó itself but ran into tougher resistance, being held up by enemy machine-gun fire. At 5.00am swimmers secured a bridgehead; they were soon followed by boats, and, with the support of the 35th Division's artillery, the defences were neutralised and work on a footbridge began at 7.00am. Soon work could begin on a larger bridge at Ascó and Colonel Modesto was to locate his headquarters in a railway tunnel here. Meanwhile diversionary crossings were carried out up- and downstream to draw away Rebel forces and mask the true intention of the offensive. In one such effort, some 50 kilometres south at Amposta, the largely French 14th International Brigade quickly ran into difficulty, its attempt to cross the river ending in bloody failure and heavy casualties. Conversely, the main thrust was overwhelmingly successful and through 25 July V and XV Corps drove on towards Gandesa. The 13th Brigade built on its initial success and pushed to Corbera, destroying the 5th *Tabor* of *Regulares* of the 13th Division which had rapidly deployed to defend the town. The 11th International Brigade was soon advancing even further ahead while the 15th Brigade crossed the river as the 35th Division's reserve. The Internationals under Valledor had achieved the largest advance of any Loyalist troops that day. Modesto had accomplished the Republic's greatest military feat of the war: his forces had created a 70-kilometre breach in the Rebel lines, captured 800 square kilometres of enemy territory in a single day, and the 12th February battalion of the 11th International Brigade was tantalisingly close to the operation's final objective, having reached the cemetery of Gandesa, just half a kilometre north of the town, at dusk. However, logistical problems beset the offensive from the get-go. As soon as it became apparent what was transpiring, the Nationalists opened locks further up the river, causing surges of fast-flowing water that swept away pontoons and ferries and damaged bridges. By the battle's first afternoon the Rebels had also established air superiority and hammered the Ebro crossings constantly, frequently forcing bridges to close for repairs. Pre-existing congestion on the Republican bank was only aggravated by this Nationalist interdiction and as a result supplies of food, water, ammunition and heavy weapons only made it across the river in dribs and drabs. Very quickly the Republican attacking momentum drained away. Troops had to waste valuable hours foraging for food and water in temperatures that daily exceeded 30 °C. It was not until 27 July that the first heavy support could cross in the form of three tanks and some corps artillery; for the first three days of the battle the Loyalist infantry had been unsupported in assaulting defensive positions.

Gandesa marked the boundary line between the Republican XV Corps to the north and V Corps to the south, and the 35th and 11th Divisions of the two respective corps would be engaged for the next nine days in trying to seize the town. Nationalist command had recognised the importance of this crucial road junction on 25 July, and ordered numerous units of the 13th and 74th Divisions to march through the night to ensure Gandesa did not fall the following day. One such unit was the 4th Bandera of the Foreign Legion, which undertook a forced march from south of Amposta and at around 2.00am on 26 July forced its way into the Gandesa cemetery. The population was mobilised to build barricades and dig anti-tank ditches and trenches outside the town. Nationalist support troops such as mule drivers and clerks were pressed into front-line service. By 8.00am three more Foreign Legion Banderas, the 5th, 6th and 16th, had arrived. Additionally, four Tabors of Moroccans would eventually be

Veteran Brigader Joe Brandt of the Lincoln-Washingtons in action at Corbera in July 1938, armed with a Czech Mauser. (*Tamiment Library and Robert F. Wagner Labor Archive*)

Disaster: The French crossing of the Ebro

Thanks to a combination of poor intelligence, difficult terrain and the alertness of the defending forces (which nullified the surprise achieved further north), the 14th International Brigade's crossing of the Ebro ended in total disaster. The largely French–Belgian 14th *La Marseillaise* Brigade represented the southernmost element of the Ebro offensive and undertook three crossings around Amposta as a diversion for the main thrust further north. Kahle's 45th Division, consisting of the 12th and 14th International Brigades, was tasked as the reserve for V Corps, as it appears Republican high command was well aware of the poor combat record of both units, the 12th Garibaldis having gone into severe decline after their glorious defeat of the CTV at Guadalajara. Hubert's 14th Brigade was not a little disadvantaged by lack of support, given that V Corps had concentrated its artillery for the main assault and this diversionary action received the assistance only of some aged coastal guns. The Vaillant-Couturier battalion attacked first, furthest east. At 00.30am on 25 July the battalion's vanguard crossed to the island of Gracía, a small islet in the centre of the river. On reaching the island, the volunteers were met with a hail of machine-gun fire from the Nationalist bank, which holed and sank many of the boats. Of the one hundred men who had crossed, only forty are said to have returned and the battalion's commander, the French-Algerian René Cazala, was killed. Further upstream, west of Amposta, the effort of the André Marty

Standard of the Commune de Paris battalion, oldest of the French International brigade units. (*Wikimedia user Manuchansu, CC BY-SA 3.0*)

The Ebro crossing. (*Tamiment Library and Robert F. Wagner Labor Archive*)

battalion was over before it had even begun as hand grenades and machine-gun fire ended the crossing attempt almost immediately. The greatest tragedy, however, was to befall the veteran Commune de Paris battalion, which had fought at University City. Near the village of Campredó, a few kilometres further upstream, the initial successful assault at 1.30am by swimmers armed with grenades was followed up by a wave of boats. The Commune battalion, with the Henri Barbusse battalion providing support fire from the opposite bank, established a bridgehead 2 kilometres wide and several hundred metres deep. However, their advance was halted by a substantial obstacle in the form of an irrigation canal, the presence of which came as a total shock to the Brigaders. At 6.00am Nationalist artillery destroyed the pontoon that had been erected and, with dawn breaking, the Commune de Paris troops found themselves trapped in a tiny pocket, with the canal (and the enemy) in front, the river behind. The Rebel 2nd Brigade of the 105th Division soon had five battalions plus a *Tabor* of *Regulares* pushing back against the French bridge-head. A withdrawal across the Ebro was impossible in broad daylight and an attempt by the André Marty battalion in mid-afternoon to cross and provide support was soon frustrated by enemy fire. The last survivors of the 1,000-strong Paris battalion, reportedly only 100 men, swam to safety at around 6.00pm, having no option but to leave their wounded comrades on the enemy bank. The Nationalists reportedly lost just 200 men in the action.

deployed in the sector. Gandesa very swiftly became a well defended, for-tified hardpoint, held by elite Francoist troops. Two heights, around 2 kilo-metres south-east of Gandesa, dominate the town and its approaches. The easternmost, Pic de l'Àliga, was taken by the arriving 15th Brigade at dawn on 26 July. However, just a few hundred metres to the west lay Hill 481, a coverless 'pimple' that would prove a tougher obstacle and came to be known by Republican troops as 'Death Hill'. Further south, the attempts of V Corps' 11th Division, the famous Lísters, to cut off Gandesa by taking Prat del Comte were frustrated. On the other hand, by noon the 13th Dombrowski brigade had managed to cut the road north of the town to Vilalba dels Arcs, although other troops of XV Corps would fail in their attempts to seize the latter. Throughout the morning of 26 July the 11th Thälmann Brigade had made repeated frontal assaults on the town but all ended in failure. The frustrations of the day were compounded when, at dawn on 27 July, two companies of Foreign Legionnaires of the 6th Bandera seized the Pic de l'Àliga from the Mackenzie-Papineaus. The effort to take it back only served to delay the assault on the higher 'Death Hill', allowing time for the Bandera to dig in and erect strong barbed-wire defences. Under constant harassment from the air at the river crossings, Republican logistics had broken down almost as soon as the offensive began, severely hampering the fighting power of the advanced troops. The need to forage for food and water on a daily basis both tired out and demoralised the men and slowed down the attacking impetus. The lack of artillery support was keenly felt in the assault on Gandesa. The wounded could not be evacuated to hospitals, which were on the other side of the river. Fred Thomas of the 15th Brigade Anti-Tank battery recorded in his diary on 27 July:

> I'm afraid we still have not got Gandesa, largely owing to our lack of artillery and tanks. The river crossing is causing a lot of trouble. The Medical Services, too, can't cope with the wounded, due to lack of ambulances. Both ferry and brigade are too often out of action.
>
> Nothing but bloody avion [aircraft] the whole day ... Vitally urgent that they get another bridge across the river, though. We have few tanks here. Also, food trucks have not been able to get over yet, and we are subsisting on captured carne (meat ... tinned) and marma-lade, but without bread ...[40]

Meanwhile, the 15th International Brigade, minus the Lincolns who were supporting the attack on Vilalba, spent a week assaulting 'Death Hill'

An International machine-gun team provides covering fire during the attack on Gandesa, using the excellent Maxim-Tokarev. (*Tamiment Library and Robert F. Wagner Labor Archive*)

south of Gandesa. Hill 481 was a steep height, devoid of cover, and attackers not only came under fire from the Legionnaires defending the hill, but also had to contend with enfilading fire from the valley and town itself. The slopes of the 'Pimple' became a living hell for the Brigaders, with the British battalion alone assaulting the height no fewer than seven times without success. In each effort, once it became clear that the attack was not going to seize the summit, the Internationals had no choice but to go to ground and suffer nerve-shredding hours of clinging to the earth, waiting for nightfall before withdrawing to safety. Equally, there was no opportunity to evacuate the wounded, given how exposed the hillside was to hostile fire. British volunteer Walter Gregory had the misfortune of leading one such attack, in which he would be shot in the neck:

> Just before dawn we started our cautious ascent, crawling from rock to rock, keeping as low as possible, and trying to leave the loose shale undisturbed, lest the sound of cascading rock fragments alert the enemy to our presence. We had moved but a short distance beyond

our own front line when we were greeted by a fusillade of rifle and machine-gun fire and any semblance of an orderly advance disappeared as each man sought cover for himself. John Angus, who was acting as the Company Commander and was a lieutenant like myself, was wounded and, as the senior officer, I took command. There was nothing that I could do to regain the momentum of our attack, as we were now pinned down by continuous enemy fire; it was now simply a matter of returning fire whenever each man thought that it was safe enough for him to expose himself for as long as it took to discharge a few rounds of ammunition at the heights above. If we could not move forward without inviting instant death, then nor could we retreat without presenting an inviting target. All we could do was stay put and wait for nightfall. What a prospect! Twelve hours of lying on rocky soil, every fragment of which seemed intent on burying itself in our bodies, of being continually shot at, of having nothing to eat or drink, of being driven half-mad by the ceaseless attention of the most malevolent flies in the whole of Spain, and of hoping that by staying still the attention of a Fascist marksman would be distracted by movement elsewhere.[41]

On 29 July the 16th Division relieved the 11th International Brigade and Modesto ordered a more ambitious flanking plan for the following day, which was to be an attempt to bring the Gandesa battle to a conclusion once and for all. The Republicans had, at least on paper, the support of twenty-two tanks and seventy-two guns, although according to XV Corps commander Manuel Tagüeña many of the aged artillery pieces were inoperable after intense usage in the early stages of the offensive. It also seems unlikely that all this heavy equipment, and the necessary ammunition, could have made it across the Ebro so quickly. Additionally, four Nationalist divisions were now in place in the sector. The plan was for the Internationals of the 35th Division to continue their frontal assaults, including on Hill 481, to keep the defenders occupied. Meanwhile the 16th Division would sweep north of the town and the 11th Division to the south in order to complete an envelopment. On 30 July, north of Gandesa, the Dombrowskis succeeded in taking the road linking the town to Tarragona and by noon on the following day they were at the Agricultural Union on the outskirts. However, they got no further. The Mackenzie-Papineaus made it to within sight of the football pitch on the town's edge. At the same time the 16th Division broke through to the cemetery, but a

An International looks out over the hills above Gandesa, which became a killing ground for Republican forces. (*Tamiment Library and Robert F. Wagner Labor Archive*)

swift Rebel counter-attack threw them back. In truth, this would be the closest the offensive would get to the decisive breakthrough. On the same day the 11th Division, supported by armour, broke through south-east of Gandesa to cut the southbound road, but a similar tank assault on the 31st was repulsed. The 15th Brigade kept up its frontal attacks, including on Hill 481, with the 13th Brigade having to be brought in to take over the push at the start of August, but no success was achieved. The repeated attacks served only to inflict ever-higher casualties on the Republican troops for ever-diminishing returns. Heavy losses were sustained by the International Brigades, with casualties particularly high among the experienced and committed men in the officer and NCO ranks. This was in no small part due to the fact that, according to Bessie, a number of the Spanish conscripts and dissatisfied Brigaders actually refused to go over the top during the battle, or else went to ground or simply disappeared during combat. One of many key figures lost as the International Brigades were asked to do nothing other than pin down the Nationalist garrison was Lewis Clive, a descendant of the eighteenth-century general Clive of

India. Clive was also a Labour party councillor and, before he joined the Brigades, an officer in the Grenadier Guards:

> Lewis Clive excelled himself as company commander. He was everywhere: directing, organising, encouraging. One morning he selected three of us to take up vantage points on a ridge facing the fascists. We were instructed to keep up a constant rifle fire on their position.
>
> I was in a rather exposed spot; my only cover a gorse bush. I concentrated my aim on a movement I detected at the base of an enemy pill-box and fired round after round until my rifle bolt became almost too hot to handle.
>
> Lewis Clive re-appeared and asked about the activity in the fascist lines. It was a hot, sunny day and, as usual, my shirtsleeves were rolled up. At that moment I felt splashes on my forearm, and glancing down, was astonished to see they were splashes of blood. Turning, I saw Lewis reel and fall. Someone below said, 'What a ghastly sight.'
>
> I slid down from my firing position and saw that the top of his head was severed completely and, as he lay there, the brain was spilling from its case. It was indeed a ghastly sight.[42]

A Lincoln-Washington light machine-gun team in action, July 1938. They are equipped with a Wz. 28, a Polish copy of the American BAR, a weapon that would see extensive use in the Second World War. (*Tamiment Library and Robert F. Wagner Labor Archive*)

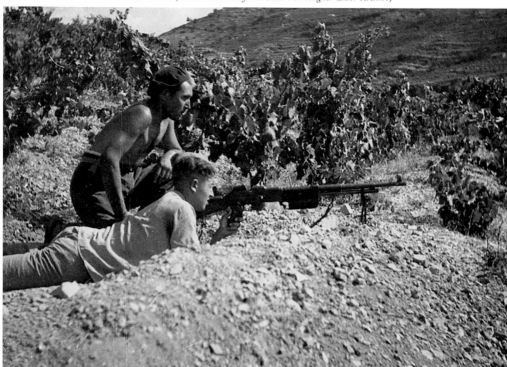

There would be no more replacements coming from abroad to replace the 'commissar material' that was sacrificed on Death Hill and elsewhere. Ultimately, none of the thrusts achieved a significant breakthrough and after five days of bitter fighting, little progress was made. The final attempt to storm the town had decimated the best units in the People's Army.

Elsewhere, the advance had also stalled, and the effort put into taking Gandesa had worn out the offensive's attacking capabilities. On 3 August 1938 Modesto finally called time on the Republic's last major operation, switching the Army of the Ebro onto a defensive footing. Perhaps Modesto should have realised his men were too tired to undertake such an ambitious attack, and the enemy too well entrenched to be overcome. However, given that it was the central objective of General Rojo's plan for the Ebro operation, at least in its first phase, the young commander's determination to seize Gandesa is understandable. Additionally, it is unclear if the largely inexperienced troops that made up the Army of the Ebro were capable of the complex manoeuvres involved, and the lack of heavy fire support caused by the enemy bombardment of the river crossings made it difficult to execute the ambitious plans. Certainly, high command underestimated the disastrous logistical difficulties that would quickly drain away the offensive's momentum. It must be said that the Nationalists also suffered huge losses in the titanic struggle for Gandesa. The 4th Bandera of the Foreign Legion sustained over 600 casualties from a strength of 1,000 men and was forced to take 750 reinforcements from an internment camp of Republican deserters and prisoners of war – ironically, a move not dissimilar to the desperate measures taken to keep the Loyalist elite, the International Brigades, in the fight. The Internationals themselves had suffered heavily after once again being used as the shock troops in a major offensive. According to Fred Thomas' diary, the Lincoln-Washingtons had suffered over 200 casualties fighting around Vilalba dels Arcs, while the British had lost 250 and the 15th Brigade's Spanish battalion 150 at Gandesa. The Army of the Ebro as a whole had suffered 12,000 casualties up to 3 August but had captured 5,000 Nationalists and inflicted considerable losses on elite enemy troops. However, the army was now totally exhausted, and Franco was building up a huge force by transferring troops from other sectors to the Ebro front, especially from the cancelled drive on Valencia. It was inevitable that a counter-attack was coming and the Republican commissars could only motivate the demoralised men with exhortations to simply hold the territory they had taken.

Milton Wolff and the American volunteers

Affectionately known as *El Lobo* to his men, Milton Wolff began his service with the American volunteers as a machine-gun crew's water carrier but rose through the ranks to become commander of the Lincoln-Washington battalion. Born in 1915 and raised in Brooklyn, New York, the son of eastern European Jewish immigrants, Wolff's experience of the Great Depression shaped his politics and he became active in the 1930s in the Young Communist League. A pacifist, Wolff originally wanted to serve as a medic but was recruited into the George Washington battalion's machine-gun company and would fight at every one of the Americans' major engagements from Brunete in July 1937 onwards. The George Washington and Abraham Lincoln battalions suffered 50 per cent casualties at that battle and were merged in mid-July, creating the Lincoln-Washingtons. Wolff quickly gained a reputation for coolness in combat but also miraculous good luck, and indeed he would be one of the few International volunteers to escape without a wound, despite numerous

The lanky, bedraggled Milton Wolff (*left*), while still a machine-gunner, posing with his Maxim M1910 and fellow crewmen in 1937. (*Tamiment Library and Robert F. Wagner Labor Archive*)

instances of men being hit just inches from him. In the disaster of the Great Retreats, many men ended up lost, captured or killed, and Wolff found himself wandering alone through Nationalist territory for several days before swimming back to safety across the Ebro. As the battalion was rebuilt, Wolff was promoted to command the Lincolns, although he would later admit that despite his personal bravery, extensive combat experience and booming voice, he lacked the training for military command and was bewildered by the unexpected tasks he faced, such as where to locate the battalion armoury. Nevertheless, he led the battalion back across the Ebro in July 1938 and the men fought bravely in their final battles under his leadership.

Many former Lincolns would serve in the Second World War, although in some cases they were prevented from seeing combat or being promoted as they were labelled 'premature antifascists' by the US military. Wolff himself would work first as a recruiter for British Intelligence in the US and later for the American Office of Strategic Services (OSS) in behind-the-lines resistance operations in Europe, as he and a number of American veterans excelled in partisan operations for US intelligence. The Cold War would bring harder years, with the Brigade veterans' association banned and Wolff himself hauled in front of the Un-American Activities Committee. His autobiographical novel *Another Hill* is one of the best English-language accounts of the conflict, telling not only his own story as 'Castle' but also that of a serial deserter he knew in the battalion, 'Leo'.

The Nationalists now had 8 divisions, 300 artillery guns, 100 tanks and 500 aircraft with which to carry out their counter-offensive. With the best of the People's Army pinned down in the lower Ebro bend, with the river behind them, Franco could have used this force to drive into northern Catalonia or even carry out his own crossing to encircle the Republican salient. Instead, he chose to take the Army of the Ebro head on and to regain every metre of lost territory. The key to the whole bridgehead was the Sierra de Pàndols, a mountain range south of Gandesa which, as well as being a strong defensive position, provided observation of the entire area, allowing the Republicans to watch their opponents. Conversely,- should the Rebels capture the mountains, the Loyalist forces in the Ebro salient would be under their observation, allowing the Nationalists to direct their superior air and artillery firepower more effectively. The heights, a number of which were over 600 metres, were held by Líster's V Corps, and the veteran 11th Division specifically. The Rebel attack began on 10 August, supported by an intense three-hour artillery barrage, with the Nationalist 4th Division, supported by colonial battalions, throwing

Troops of the 15th International Brigade fighting their way up the Sierra de Pàndols, August 1938. (*Tamiment Library and Robert F. Wagner Labor Archive*)

its troops at the heights. Pounded by 9,000 tonnes of shells, the Lísters held firm. However, the Rebels did not relent and under constant air, ground and artillery attack, it was not long before the 11th Division had to be relieved, having suffered 2,500 casualties and lost two of its three brigade commanders. The 35th Division and its International Brigades were selected to take over this most crucial part of the line, highlighting how Modesto and Rojo still viewed the volunteers as among the best troops at their disposal. On 14 August the Nationalists seized Hill 705 and other heights, creating a narrow salient into the Republican line, but fanatical defence from the Lísters prevented the Rebels from making further progress. That night the 35th Division relieved the 11th and took over the defence of the Sierra de Pàndols. Their first objective was to re-establish the strong defensive lines from which the Lísters had been driven back and after a hard day's fighting the North American Mackenzie-Papineaus and Lincolns had taken back Hills 609 and 641, as well as the central Hill 666. On 16 August the whole 35th Division took up the offensive, although little was gained in the Pàndols proper. Further north, that afternoon the Edgar André, Hans Beimler and 12th February battalions of the 11th International Brigade had succeeded in taking 'Death Hill', the height at the very north of the Sierra, just south of Gandesa, which had frustrated the

British for so long. However, on 19 August they were driven off the height by the Nationalist 13th Division and withdrew half a kilometre to the Pinell de Brai road. By the following day the Thälmanns had secured their position on the Hill of Saint Mark, a large mountain north of Hill 666 and the site of a prominent church. The Pàndols proved a grim spot to garrison; it was nearly impossible to dig in on the cold, windswept, rocky cliff sides. Men and mules fell to their deaths down ravines and off sheer cliff edges, while bringing up supplies and evacuating the wounded became extremely difficult. The mountainside was too rocky to scratch out trenches more than a few feet deep and there was nothing to fill the sandbags with, so the men built primitive stone parapets for defence. The position was badly exposed to Nationalist artillery and aircraft, including the Condor Legion's Flak 88s firing over open sights, and when shells detonated on the mountainside, they sent deadly fragments of rock flying in all directions as well as shrapnel. The worst day in the heights was 19 August; a 7½-hour artillery barrage (an experience one American

Digging in was extremely difficult on the rocky sierra, as these men of the Mackenzie-Papineau battalion found out, and shellfire was made more deadly by fragments of rock being thrown in all directions. (*Tamiment Library and Robert F. Wagner Labor Archive*)

volunteer described as 'waiting like a rat in a trap') was followed up by a strong Moroccan attack, which the 15th Brigade repulsed. By this time the Rebel 4th Navarrese Division had suffered 3,800 casualties and actually had to be relieved by the 84th Division. The 15th Brigade continued to suffer heavy bombardments and take part in tit-for-tat raids, attacks and counter-attacks. The experience in the mountains was not one that would be swiftly forgotten, according to one British volunteer:

> When the massive Fascist war machine was hurled into action the British Battalion was more fortunate than other battalions of the XVth Brigade for it escaped the full force of the enemy's initial offensive. We were troubled by artillery fire which claimed a steadily mounting number of casualties but we were not so hard pressed ourselves that we could not send out companies in support of the Lincolns and the Mac Paps who were receiving a heavy mauling. We did, however, launch a successful concerted attack against an outlying spur of Hill 666 which was the key to the entire Pàndols sector.
>
> On 24th August it was our turn to feel the full weight of the Fascist advance. We had barely taken over the Lincolns' position on the main heights of the Pàndols when the enemy launched its biggest and most sustained attack yet on this sector of the front. An artillery barrage, the like of which none of us had ever experienced, crashed down around us and flying shrapnel and rock splinters inflicted dozens of minor injuries. As soon as the barrage lifted, two Fascist infantry battalions hurled themselves against us. Although still reeling from the shock waves of the barrage we stood our ground and repelled the Fascists but only after bitter fighting in which the Battalion received heavy casualties. That night we were relieved by a Spanish unit, and later we received a citation from the Brigade and the 35th Division for our efforts in holding Hill 666 against such incredibly superior odds.[43]

On the night of 25/26 August the 35th Division was relieved by the Republican 43rd Division, with the immediate threat receding. Thanks in no small part to the Brigaders' sacrifice, Loyalist forces held the Sierra de Pàndols practically until the withdrawal back across the Ebro in November 1938, hindering Nationalist operations in the sector for the duration of the battle. It had cost about half the strength of the 15th Brigade and a quarter of the 11th Brigade. As they went into their final period in reserve, those Brigaders with fourteen months' service, including at least six at the

A battery of sFH 18 heavy German howitzers supplied to the Rebels by Hitler. The Nationalist advantage in artillery made itself felt during the Ebro campaign, especially during the Francoist counter-offensive. (*Bundesarchiv*)

front, were granted leave in Paris, a concession that was seen by many hopeful volunteers as a portent of imminent repatriation.

Demobilisation

Despite their failure to take the Pàndols, the Francoist counter-offensive continued throughout August and into September, gradually grinding down the Republican defenders in battles of attrition that resembled First World War conditions. On 3 September a fresh assault began around Corbera, aimed at taking the Sierra de Caballs, a series of heights roughly 5 kilometres west of Gandesa and 1 kilometre north-west of the Sierra de Pàndols. By 5 September Corbera was in Rebel hands and, after taking some hills in the Sierra de la Vall de la Torre (a smaller range stretching north of the Caballs), the Nationalists were threatening the Caballs seriously. As a result, on 6 September first Hans Kahle's 45th Division (returned from the failed crossing at Amposta) and later the 35th were committed to the defence of this newly threatened part of the line. These units formed the core of a counter-attacking force rapidly put together by Modesto, supported by whatever tanks and artillery the Republicans could

The view from the Sierra de Pàndols made it a vital position and Republican command demanded that it be held at all costs. (*Tamiment Library and Robert F. Wagner Labor Archive*)

muster, and their efforts on 6 and 7 September halted the Nationalist advance. Intense fighting continued until the night of 10/11 September; however, the latest Rebel assault had petered out, having achieved a penetration of around 5 kilometres at the cost of 7,000 casualties. The majority of the Sierra de Caballs remained in Republican hands, albeit at the cost of 12,000 casualties. Bessie marvelled at the continued fighting spirit of the Brigades, despite the mauling they had taken in the Ebro campaign:

> Largest in your mind bulked the discrepancy between the morale of the men and the fight they had put up in this sector, the Sierra Cabals [*sic*]. Always, before action, they seemed demoralized enough to desert in droves, or at least to keep their heads down and retreat without orders. Always, when they went in, they put up a terrific resistance, and they attacked like devils. It had been the same on Hill 666 of the Sierra Pandols. But give them a few days' rest out of the lines and they would be talking about Paris leaves again, about repatriation, and griping and swearing never to go into action again.

This was a phenomenon of a rather curious nature ... The Spanish kids too ... had done a good job despite the presence in their ranks of many weak and unreliable elements.[44]

The high levels of demoralisation recorded in various accounts has led to historians writing off the International Brigades as a spent force time and again, yet they continued to be brought in to the toughest sectors of the line and to fight tooth and nail once there. In general, the Internationals did not fight like demoralised troops, even if they have given that impression in numerous reports and accounts since.

On 17 September the assault was renewed, this time the elite Rebel 13th Division striking through the Sierra de la Vall de la Torre towards Venta de Campesinos. They were opposed by the Internationals of the 45th Division, as well as the 13th Dombrowski Brigade of the 35th Division, who limited the Nationalist advance to just a kilometre on the first day, despite the Francoists enjoying substantial support from aircraft, artillery

British battalion command post in a cave in the Pàndols. Battalion commander Sam Wild (*centre, in beret*) was wounded in the hand during the battle but refused to leave for medical treatment until the Brigade was relieved. Subsequently he would be awarded the Republic's highest honour for bravery. (*Tamiment Library and Robert F. Wagner Labor Archive*)

and a company of tanks. Over the next few days the Francoists ground slowly forward, the tough Moroccan and Foreign Legion troops measuring their progress in metres and suffering immense casualties. The 13th Division's war diary recorded:

> The Tabores had to advance clearing the trenches with hand grenades every ten metres against an enemy that had not been destroyed by the repeated bombardment of our artillery concentrations.[45]

Unsurprisingly, the Internationals were taking a hammering in holding their ground against such firepower. By 20 September the 13th Division had to be relieved by the 4th Navarrese Division, a reliable Carlist unit, to maintain any sort of attacking momentum. At exactly the same time the fate of the International Brigades was being decided in Geneva. Throughout September the Republican Prime Minister Juan Negrín had been working with the conservative Duke of Alba to try to secure a negotiated peace. This was part of the wider diplomatic events overtaking Europe at that time which would conclude with the Munich Agreement later in the month, handing the Czech Sudetenland to Hitler in a vain attempt to avoid another world war. Franco rejected out of hand all peace terms save unconditional surrender. A first step towards a settlement in the form of the withdrawal of both sides' foreign volunteers was also not achieved, again due to Franco's unwillingness. Nevertheless, peace was the only card Negrín had left to play. In an attempt both to display his good faith in negotiations and to shame the Western Powers into compelling Franco to comply, on 21 September 1938 Negrín announced to the League of Nations that the International Brigades would be unilaterally withdrawn from Spain under the supervision of League observers. He had been informed by the Republican Chief of Staff General Rojo that the shattered International Brigades were no longer of significant military value, and certainly less so than the German Condor Legion and Italian CTV that were instrumental to the Nationalist war effort. Unsurprisingly, the Western democracies failed to act, and Franco did not feel inclined to match Negrín's magnanimity, offering token withdrawals but retaining his Italian and German forces until the end of the war. The Brigades were to be withdrawn regardless. It is unclear whether the Brigaders knew of this going into combat for the last time. Certainly, the officers and Brigade staff were aware of Negrín's announcement, although they tried to keep the information to themselves so that the men would not give up fighting. Many Brigader memoirs claim that they knew this would be their last battle, and it is clear that this sort of news spread fast through the ranks. The last stand of the International Brigades would be undertaken by the Lincoln, British and Mackenzie-Papineau battalions of the 15th Brigade. On 22 September they were brought up to the Venta de Campesinos sector to relieve the shattered Dombrowskis. The Lincolns had just 280 men left, 80 of whom were Americans, while the British battalion could muster 337, a third of whom were foreign volunteers. British company commander Lieutenant Walter Gregory described the desperate situation the 15th Brigade inherited:

> Ahead of us, in the Sierra del Lavall de la Torre [*sic*], the XIIIth International Brigade, Dombrowski, had taken terrible punishment. Only a few men from each of its units were still able to offer resistance when we moved into the sector of the front south of the Corbera– Venta de Camposina road. To put it bluntly our sector was in one hell of a mess. All of our positions were dominated by the higher ground which lay in Fascist hands. To our left were the Mac Paps. To our

The Internationals suffered murderous losses during the Ebro campaign.
(*Tamiment Library and Robert F. Wagner Labor Archive*)

right, and on the far side of the road, were the Lincolns. Running along beside the road was a small stream which was flanked on each side by a dense mass of canes. We began to dig trenches in the thin, stony soil but, as always our trenches afforded protection only to crouching men.[46]

Milton Wolff, commander of the Lincoln-Washington battalion, came across streams of retreating Republican troops. As they moved up late on 22 September, they

could see that they were the Dombrowskis – the Poles, Hungarians, and Palestinian Jews, European hard-fighting IB'ers of the Thirteenth Brigade. Slowly, painfully, they exchanged information in English, Spanish, Yiddish, French ... separately and all together.

The Dombrowskis had been under attack for three days and finally the lines had broken. They were going back. Back to where? Just back. Back to where someone would tell them what to do, but right now they were going back because there had been too much for them to take after all. They were going back to where there would be some rest and perhaps hot food, something they had not had for three days. Afterward, they would return to the front and fight some more. But now they were going back ...

'Take it easy, comrades,' he said to the Poles. 'We'll hold the line.'

'No. It cannot be so,' one said to him, 'there is too much against us here.'[47]

The 15th International Brigade strung out a line on Hills 365 and 361 in the Sierra de la Vall de la Torre, 4 kilometres south-west of Venta de Campesinos. The Lincolns were on the right, the British to their left (south), followed by the Mackenzie-Papineaus. On the morning of 23 September they were subjected to a five-hour artillery barrage, the intensity of which, by all accounts, was unmatched during the volunteers' entire time in Spain. First World War veterans were reminded of the Western Front. A narrow ravine ran directly back from the American lines and under the strain of the bombardment the Lincolns broke, fleeing down the convenient escape route nature had provided. Milton Wolff left his command dug-out to find, to his disbelief, his battalion's trenches unoccupied and Rebel troops flooding into their positions. Possibly, Rebel troops had infiltrated the American lines during the barrage, rendering the position untenable and triggering the retreat. Perhaps the men had simply not wished

Lincoln-Washingtons resting near Corbera, September 1938, shortly before the Brigade's final battle. (*Tamiment Library and Robert F. Wagner Labor Archive*)

to die on their final day in battle. Whatever the cause, the Lincolns' withdrawal left the flanks of the British and Canadians completely exposed. The Major Attlee company of the British battalion, in the most advanced position, was completely overrun and those who were not killed fell into National captivity. Chaos ensued as the 15th Brigade's line crumbled in the face of tank and infantry assaults. Commissar Bob Cooney recalled:

We had a warm time almost from the start. Never before had I experienced such a pounding as the enemy guns inflicted on us. The ground trembled beneath us. Almost before one shell exploded we felt the crash of the next. Our brains reeled from the concussion. The trenches we occupied had suffered from the previous day's bombardment. Today's affair threatened to destroy them entirely. At some points the parapet was blown away and we could only move along the trench by clambering over mounds of earth and rock, thus exposing ourselves to enemy infantry fire.

Towards mid-day our position became untenable. The hill on our right flank was occupied by the enemy [the Lincoln position], with the result that we came under enfilading fire from the right, gradually creeping round to our rear. The artillery bombardment intensified, and under cover of the barrage the Moors came over – a savage yelling horde. There was a hand-to-hand fight for the trench, but the result was obvious from the start. Even had we succeeded in repelling the Moors, we could have been encircled and destroyed. So we retreated in as good order as possible to the next ridge, where we took advantage of a long low natural mound to form a new line. We left a tragic number of dead behind as well as prisoners.[48]

Rallying at Brigade HQ about a kilometre further back, the Internationals were fortunate that the Nationalists did not press their advantage; a timely Loyalist artillery barrage had slowed the attacking momentum and the exhausted Rebels had called off this latest stage of Franco's incremental counter-offensive by the end of the day. At 1.00am on 24 September the bitter remnants of the final International Brigade in combat were relieved and withdrawn across the Ebro. It had been a tragic end to the long, distinguished service of the International Brigades. At roll call the British battalion had just 173 men, 74 of whom were British. Reportedly there were only 35 Mackenzie-Papineaus on their feet by the end of

CV 33s speeding across the Catalan countryside. Many Republican troops had no anti-tank weaponry whatsoever. (*Bundesarchiv*)

the day. Similarly, the Rebel 13th Division had to be withdrawn from the Ebro campaign shortly after, having suffered losses of 233 officers and 6,100 men. For the shock troops of both sides this was an unforgiving campaign. The 45th Division, with its 12th and 14th International Brigades, was relieved on 25 September, although the front was quiet by then. It would not be until 9 October that the 129th International Brigade, which had been trapped on the now static Levante Front near Valencia, was taken out of the line.

Several months of rest and recuperation in Catalonia would follow for the volunteers. They soon had to watch their Spanish comrades march back to the Ebro. The International Brigades were converted into purely Spanish mixed brigades of the People's Army, albeit without their experienced officers, NCOs and commissars, who were of course by and large Internationals. Their efforts were to be in vain, for by mid-November the Republicans had been driven back to their start lines and had recrossed the Ebro river. The front now followed exactly the same course as it had nearly four months before on 25 July. Casualty figures given for the long attritional battle vary considerably, from 40,000 on both sides to 70,000 Republican and 60,000 Nationalist. Whatever the true figure, what is clear is that the battle had consumed the last of the fighting power of the People's Army, in terms of both experienced soldiers and weapons and equipment. There was no doubt the Republic would now lose the war, despite still holding close to half the country. Hopes for international intervention to mediate a peace had disappeared after the Munich agreement, the high-water mark of appeasement. All the while, the Internationals attended various banquets and ceremonies to give thanks to the International Brigades as they waited, rather frustrated, to be allowed to leave. The celebrations were to culminate on Friday, 28 October with a lavish parade of thousands of Internationals through Barcelona, the beating heart of the Spanish revolution. All Brigaders present reported being swept up in the emotion of the occasion, as is clear in the diary of Fred Thomas:

> Yesterday was a day I will never forget. The Parade was, I am sure, an emotional feast for us all. It was no simple march through the streets, but a glorious demonstration of the enthusiasm and affection of the people of Catalonia for the Internationals.
>
> Trucks took us through crowded streets, with flags and bunting everywhere, the people cheering and throwing flowers, crowding

Commander: Sam Wild

Sam Wild was a tough Mancunian born in 1908 into an Irish immigrant working-class family. He served for a time in the Royal Navy, but this only made him 'anti-King, anti-ruling class, [and] anti-officer' and on his discharge he became politically active with the unemployed workers' movement. His left-wing politics were firmly rooted, despite coming from a conservative, Catholic family:

> I was always Labour, even as a ten-year-old kid. I can remember being in an argument with a kid at the top of the street round about election time . . . I'd gained a reputation in the Navy of being a Bolshie. I'd taken an interest in what was going on in Russia, the struggle of the Irish people for home rule, and the General Strike.
>
> (Corkill & Rawnsley (eds), 1981, pp. 16–17.)

Arriving in Spain in January 1937, Wild fought in all the British battalion's major battles, being wounded five times and gaining an unrivalled reputation for bravery. Having commanded the Major Attlee company, in January 1938 he took over the battalion. He became, in the opinion of many, the best British battalion commander of the war, with a 'special genius' for command, leading by example and trusted by his men. Wild did, however, suffer from a drink problem and was noted for the extremity of his language when dealing with subordinates. Nevertheless, he 'behaved like a real first class British officer in battle' and perhaps his leadership explains in part the willingness of the British battalion to go over the top time and again at Hill 481, 'Death Hill'. Wild ended the war a major and was decorated with the Republic's highest award for bravery, but on his return home he was barred from serving in even the Home Guard during the Second World War, owing to his politics. Wild in many ways embodies the officer class of the International Brigades: brave, leading from the front, ideologically devout, but tactically naïve.

Sam Wild (*centre*), flanked by Spaniards of the British battalion.

every window and balcony. We dismounted finally at the Sarria Road, starting point of the procession.

There the Brigades of many different nationalities were drawn up nine abreast. Spanish troops lined the route as, led by military bands, we set off. Everywhere thousands packed the broad streets, time after time men and women broke through the cordon to hug and kiss us, holding up small children and babies to be kissed in return, smothering us with affection as they cheered and cheered.

For an hour and a half we made our slow way through some of the principle [*sic*] streets in one long glut of emotional excess. I was not the only Brigader sometimes reduced to tears: we, who were leaving the fight, were yet receiving the heartfelt homage of the Spanish people.

In the Street of the 14th of April the march ended, and then came the speeches. From a platform full of important people from many countries as well as of the Republic, Dr Negrin, Prime Minister,

Territorial division of Spain in February 1939, after the fall of Catalonia. Republican-held territory is dark, Nationalist light. (*Wikimedia User Nordnordwest, CC BY-SA 3.0*)

addressed us and the vast crowds. Then came President Azaña followed by the Chief of the Army of the Ebro. Finally we recognised the spare figure of the indomitable 'La Pasionaria' who quickly had the crowd roaring their approval of her every word.[49]

The parade culminated with a rip-roaring speech from Dolores Ibárruri, better known as *La Pasionaria*, Spain's most famous Communist. Her speech would go down in International Brigade folklore, and still resonates decades later, perhaps because *La Pasionaria*'s words, unlike some Comintern agitprop, were so heartfelt:

> It is very difficult to say a few words in farewell to the heroes of the International Brigades, because of what they are and what they represent. A feeling of sorrow, an infinite grief catches our throat – sorrow for those who are going away … grief for those who will stay here for ever mingled with the Spanish soil …
>
> From all peoples, from all races, you came to us like brothers, like sons of immortal Spain; and in the hardest days of the war, when the capital of the Spanish Republic was threatened, it was you, gallant comrades of the International Brigades, who helped save the city with your fighting enthusiasm, your heroism and your spirit of sacrifice.

The farewell parade to the International Brigades. (*RGASPI*)

And Jarama and Guadalajara, Brunete and Belchite, Levante and the Ebro, in immortal verses sing of the courage, the sacrifice, the daring, the discipline of the men of the International Brigades.

For the first time in the history of the peoples' struggles, there was the spectacle, breath-taking in its grandeur, of the formation of International Brigades to help save a threatened country's freedom and independence – the freedom and independence of our Spanish land.

Communists, Socialists, Anarchists, Republicans – men of different colours, differing ideology, antagonistic religions – yet all profoundly loving liberty and justice, they came and offered themselves to us unconditionally.

They gave us everything – their youth or their maturity; their science or their experience; their blood and their lives; their hopes and aspirations – and they asked us for nothing. But yes, it must be said, they did want a post in battle, they aspired to the honor of dying for us.

Banners of Spain! Salute these many heroes! Be lowered to honour so many martyrs!

Mothers! Women! When the years pass and the wounds of war are stanched; when the memory of the sad and bloody days disappears in a present of liberty, of peace and of well-being; when the feelings of rancour have died out and pride in a free country is felt equally by all Spaniards, speak to your children. Tell them of these men of the International Brigades.

Tell them how, coming over seas and mountains, crossing frontiers bristling with bayonets ... these men reached our country as crusaders for freedom, to fight and die for Spain's liberty and independence threatened by German and Italian fascism. They gave up everything – their loves, their countries, home and fortune, fathers, mothers, wives, brothers, sisters and children – and they came and said to us: 'We are here. Your cause, Spain's cause, is ours. It is the cause of all advanced and progressive mankind.'

Today many are departing. Thousands remain, shrouded in Spanish earth, profoundly remembered by all Spaniards. Comrades of the International Brigades: political reasons, reasons of state, the welfare of that very cause for which you offered your blood with boundless generosity, are sending you back, some to your own countries and others to forced exile. You can go proudly. You are

An emotional, wounded Brigader gives the clenched fist salute during the farewell speeches. Robert Capa's photos of the event remain some of the most famous images of the war. (© *Robert Capa* © *International Center of Photography/Magnum Photos*)

history. You are legend. You are the heroic example of democracy's solidarity and universality ...

We shall not forget you; and, when the olive tree of peace is in flower, entwined with the victory laurels of the Republic of Spain – come back!

Return to our side for here you will find a homeland – those who have no country ... who must live deprived of friendship – all, all will have the affection and gratitude of the Spanish people who today and tomorrow will shout with enthusiasm – Long live the heroes of the International Brigades!

Conclusion

You are Legend

On 14 October the International Commission for the Withdrawal of Volunteers was established at Perpignan, just over the French frontier. Its role was to register all International Brigade personnel, whether in the rest areas, hospitals or PoWs, and oversee their removal from Spain, including to their final destinations. The lengthy bureaucratic processes this entailed meant that the volunteers did not leave until December 1938 and January 1939. For many of the Internationals, for instance those from Germany, Austria, Italy, Poland or Yugoslavia, there was no chance of returning home because of the right-wing or fascist dictatorships established in their own nations. Service in Spain must have been particularly dislocating for Austrian volunteers, for their homeland had ceased to exist in March 1938, annexed by Nazi Germany. An uncertain future awaited these displaced Brigaders, along with the 500,000 Republican refugees who streamed across the French frontier in January 1939 as Franco swiftly conquered Catalonia. Some 6,000 Brigaders were either denied entry to France or else opted to stay and fight as individuals, and served in the desperate but futile defence of Catalonia. The attack began on 23 December 1938 and by late January 1939 the Nationalists had seized Spain's economic heartland; the People's Army was broken in spirit and without enough rifles to arm its men. The Republicans who did make it over the frontier, both Spaniards and Brigaders unable to go home, were held in internment camps across southern France. The provision at these camps was rudimentary at best and some of them were simply open-air enclosures on beaches or in fields. The Spanish Republic, for whom the Brigaders had fought so hard, was to disappear soon after their departure. In January and February 1939 Republican unity began to fracture in the face of certain defeat. The central zone of the Republic still constituted 30 per cent of Spain but stocks of food and munitions were running perilously low. Prime Minister Negrín fled into France as Catalonia fell, but flew back to Republican territory, only for his President, Manuel Azaña, and Chief of the General Staff Rojo to refuse to do the same. Negrín's policy was continued resistance to buy time for a general evacuation (although he did not let the latter be known to prevent panic) as his secret approaches to Franco and attempts to enlist international mediators had failed. As one of the few remaining reliable officers, Modesto was promoted to general and appointed head of the central front, replacing Colonel Casado, a Loyalist professional officer. Casado and a cabal of People's Army officers (which included Miaja, the 'Hero of Madrid'), Anarchists, Socialists and Franco sympathisers, then launched an anti-Communist coup in March aimed at ousting Negrín and negotiating a peace with the Nationalists. After a short 'civil war within the civil war', Negrín was forced to flee and the Casado junta tried, in vain, to appeal to Franco's soldierly honour. Unsurprisingly, the Generalissimo was not interested in negotiation and in late March began his final offensive, facing little opposition, with the Republican army aware that its leaders had asked for peace. On 1 April 1939 Francisco Franco declared the Spanish Civil War over. There would be little mercy for the defeated: concentration camps, prisons, forced labour, black lists and even execution awaited those who could not get away.

This is not the place to recount the experiences of the volunteers after Spain, which has been done already in great detail in many national

The conditions in the internment camps on France's Mediterranean coast were at times appalling, with no protection from the elements. Some Brigaders and Spanish Republicans spent years in these camps before being handed over to the Nazis.

Nationalist forces advancing against no opposition as the Republic falls apart, March 1939. (*Bundesarchiv*)

Franco's troops enter Madrid without a fight, over two years after the Internationals' heroic stand to defend the city. (*Shutterstock, Everett Historical 251930548*)

Franco's legacy: one of countless mass graves of Republicans executed by the Nationalists, discovered in 2014. (*Wikimedia Mario Modesto Mata CC BY-SA 4.0*)

studies of the Brigades. Unsurprisingly, a huge number went on to serve in the Second World War. Some Americans and British were prevented from either joining up or being promoted because of their service in the civil war, being viewed as politically suspect. However, many served their country with distinction, a number of US volunteers being recruited into the Office of Strategic Services (OSS), forerunner to the Central Intelligence Agency (CIA), and taking part in behind-the-lines activities in occupied Europe. In particular, European veterans of the International Brigades became prominent in their national resistance movements. Luigi Longo, or Gallo as he was known in Spain, was the leader of the highly effective Italian resistance movement. Colonel Rol-Tanguy, former commissar and battalion commander in the 14th Brigade, became a national hero, leading the Paris resistance uprising which helped liberate the city in August 1944. That liberation was carried out by Free French forces, among whose commanders was former Brigader Joseph Putz, whose French Foreign Legion troops contained hundreds of Spanish Republicans who had opted for military service as a way out of internment. Josip Tito's Yugoslav partisans included many veterans of the International Brigades,

Former 14th International Brigade officer Colonel Rol-Tanguy became a national hero in France as a resistance leader. Pictured is the plaque at the Paris metro station on Avenue du Colonel Henri Rol-Tanguy. (*Author's photograph*)

while the future president himself had actually worked to recruit International Brigaders during the civil war. The unpopular French officer Jules Dumont was arrested for his resistance activities and executed by the Gestapo in 1942. Several thousand volunteers interred by the French at the end of the civil war fell into Nazi hands after the fall of France. They met a grisly fate in the German concentration camp system. A large number, as well as thousands of Spanish Republicans, were imprisoned at the Mauthausen concentration camp, where as many as 300,000 people died. One Garibaldi volunteer, Bertolini, described the experience of the camps to Alvah Bessie forty years later:

> I spent four and a half years in the French concentration camp at Le Vernet ... Then they handed me over to the Nazis who put me in Buchenwald for the next twenty-one months. A secret military organisation inside Buchenwald, of which Bertolini was one leader, helped to liberate those wretched prisoners before the US Army entered Weimar.[50]

Many never made it out of the camps, such as former Polish commander Stanislaw Ulanowski, who died in Gross-Rosen in 1944.

In the post-war world the fate of the Brigaders was mixed. In the United States the Cold War and the birth of McCarthyism resulted in many veterans facing blacklisting or criminal charges and subsequent spells in prison, while in Eastern Europe, where Communist regimes were installed by the Soviets, the Internationals were revered as heroes and many attained high political or military office. Far fewer Brigade veterans could match their success in the democratic West, but Jack Jones became one of Britain's leading trade union leaders, Pacciardi served as defence minister of Italy, and more still became members of their respective parliaments or key figures in national Communist parties. The worst fate of all befell Red Army and Comintern personnel who would become victims of Stalin's Great Purges, where the likes of Kléber and Ćopić were either thrown into gulags or shot by the NKVD for reasons that were clear only to the delusional Soviet dictator. These victims were rehabilitated, posthumously, during the de-Stalinisation process of the late 1950s. *La Pasionaria*'s promise that the Brigaders would be welcomed back to a free Spain was finally fulfilled in 2009, seventy years after the end of the civil war, when the few surviving veterans were granted a Spanish passport by the Socialist government. The last surviving British volunteer, Geoffrey Servante, used his citizenship to vote in the Catalan independence refer-

An M3 halftrack of the type used by the Free French 2nd Armoured Division. The first Allied troops into Paris in 1944 were largely Spanish Republicans of the division's mechanized infantry, under the command of International Brigade veteran Joseph Putz. Their halftracks bore civil war monikers, such as 'Madrid' (*pictured*). Also note the Republican flag. (*Author's photograph*)

In the communist bloc International Brigaders were celebrated as heroes and many rose to high office. Hans Beimler, a commissar killed at University City in 1936, was one of the German volunteers celebrated on East German postage stamps.

endum of 2017. To the author's knowledge, the only remaining International Brigader at the time of writing is the 100-year-old Josep Almudéver Mateu, born in France but raised in Spain. The International Brigades will very soon entirely pass out of living memory and into history and legend.

What did the Internationals contribute to the Republican cause? In terms of casualties, we only have definite figures up to April 1938. Statistics compiled by the International Brigade base at Albacete show that 4,575 foreign volunteers had been killed in Spain to that point, with a further 5,062 severely wounded. At the Battle of the Ebro at least 1,500 more Internationals must have become casualties, to give a rather conservative estimate. Given that around 32,000 served the Republic, this gives a permanent losses rate of between 30 and 50 per cent, a total somewhere between 11,000 and 15,000. But this does not even factor in the Brigaders who chose to remain and fight on after demobilisation. Hooton quotes figures of total International Brigade casualties of 55,161, with 17,620 dead or missing. This includes the tens of thousands of Spanish troops who served in International units, both conscripts and volunteers. Regrettably, the Comintern reports provide no numbers for Spaniards serving in the Brigades. Yet from the above figures we can reasonably conclude that perhaps up to 44,000 Spaniards became casualties fighting alongside their International comrades in the ranks of the International Brigades. This higher figure is largely explained by the fact that whenever the Brigades suffered heavy losses, the ranks were refilled with Spaniards for the most part, and of course from mid-1937 onwards the International Brigades were majority Spanish.

The International Brigades were a Comintern army in the sense that a majority of volunteers were Communist Party members recruited and delivered to Spain by their national parties, and once in Spain the organisation and infrastructure of the Brigades were run by the Comintern. Yet it is decidedly unclear that this 'Communist foreign legion' was fighting for global revolution. To come to this conclusion would defy the historical record, both in terms of the volunteers' own words (whether given at the time or in later decades) and the fact that a significant minority of Internationals were non-Communist, including the majority of some national

Survivors of Mauthausen concentration camp, where a significant number of Spanish Republicans and Internationals were held, welcome the arrival of US forces in 1945 with the anti-fascist salute.

The memorial to the International Brigades at the Madrid University City campus. Unfortunately it has been vandalised on numerous occasions by far-right activists.

groups, such as Yugoslavs and Italians. The motivations that stand out most clearly across almost all volunteer groups were a commitment to the Republican cause and fervent anti-fascism. In the mid-1930s both were unifying forces on the left. Historians discount their primary sources at their peril and revolutionary zeal is decidedly lacking in such Brigade sources – hardly surprising when it is remembered that the party line in Spain was against social revolution and in favour of democracy and law and order. Even loyal Communists who served in Spain therefore parked their radical ambitions for the cause, a cause the party believed was best served through an alliance of all democrats and Leftists. Modern scholars, most convincingly the American conservative historian Stanley Payne, have debunked the Cold War theory that the Soviets were seeking to establish a satellite state in Spain and, with this in mind, it is self-evident that the volunteers' fight in Spain was an attempt to preserve Republican democracy rather than establish the dictatorship of the proletariat.

A number of historians have expressed harsh judgements about the International Brigades as combat units. In recent military histories of the war Esdaile has asserted that the Internationals 'contributed very little', while Hooton describes the volunteers as 'cannon fodder' and labels the Brigades the most cynical publicity stunt since the Children's Crusade – a frankly bizarre and inaccurate comparison, not least because the said crusade had nothing to do with publicity. Likely, Hooton is alluding to the fact that the children were said to have been tricked into sailing to what they thought was the Holy Land but was in fact a slave market. It is difficult to understand how the Brigaders were tricked, given how highly political most of them were and how recently the brutality of industrial-ised warfare had been revealed in the First World War. They were under no illusions as to what they were getting themselves into and why, and to compare their service to slavery is insulting to say the least. More justi-fiably, these historians have attempted to reassert the essential 'Spanish-ness' of the civil war and counter the overly romanticised accounts of the Brigades. However, there is a compromise position between International Brigade propaganda and writing off the Internationals entirely, a position this volume has attempted to set out. The Brigades certainly did contri-bute militarily, as we have seen throughout their story. Different Brigades performed to different levels at different stages of the war, but the Loyalist commanders trusted them and they continued to fight bravely, if not always effectively, to the end of their existence. Crucially, the Interna-tional Brigades' flaws must be seen within the context of the Republican

People's Army, for most of the defects commonly listed for the Brigades were in fact problems with the Republican Army as a whole, rather than the International units specifically. Historians are right to point out that the International Brigades suffered from poor leadership, mismanagement, overly oppressive and bureaucratic command structures, haphazard communication and coordination with other units, high levels of demoralisation and desertion, poor tactics and shoddy equipment. But all these issues were systemic flaws in the People's Army more widely, not exclusively International Brigade defects. In fact, most International Brigades and their divisions were commanded by men with far greater military experience than those leading the Spanish Republican units – many in International Brigade leadership positions had fought in the First World War, and their experience could not be matched even among the few professional officers who served the Republic, given Spain's neutrality in the First World War. There can be little doubt that training was criminally poor but at the same time it was superior to that received by the Spaniards in the People's Army; in the winter of 1936/7 the militias had no training at all, and the Internationals a few days or weeks; in 1937–8 volunteers received up to two months' or more training, while some conscripts in the People's Army found themselves at the front a fortnight after being called up. The Republican forces were desperately short of quality equipment, but the Internationals were prioritised for what little quality materiel did come through, such as the 45mm AT guns, DP28 machine guns and Czech Mauser rifles. Finally, it cannot be contested that the Brigaders were, on the whole, highly committed to the Republican cause, with a majority of volunteers being card-carrying Communists. In contrast, a majority within many other People's Army units were conscripts, for whom the war meant little, with some in fact being sympathetic to the Nationalists. It is therefore hard to maintain the argument that the International Brigades were mere cannon fodder when they were, by and large, better trained, equipped and led, not to mention significantly more motivated, than the rank and file of the People's Army. By the standards of a professional military they were hardly up to scratch, but in the specific context of the improvised People's Army and the context of a civil war fought by hastily constructed citizen militias, the International Brigades were the elite. It is true that the military efficiency of the Brigades declined over time, while that of regular People's Army units generally rose (at least until the Great Retreats of the spring of 1938). However, this was due above all to the dilution of the foreign units with

an increasing number, and eventually a majority, of the very same conscripts who limited the effectiveness of other formations. While the International Brigades were rapidly worn out thanks to constant battle and a
limited pool of volunteers, Spanish units could gradually improve over
time through greater military discipline following the militarisation of the
militias and of course access to ready replacements. Only in as dysfunc-
tional an army as that which the Republic was forced to build ad hoc in
the midst of a civil war, while under international blockade, could the
International Brigades ever represent an elite. While the leading historian
of the Republican army, Michael Alpert, plays down the significance of
the Brigades overall, his final words on the International Brigaders reveal
their true worth:

> Though they took part in most of the great battles of the Spanish Civil
> War and suffered huge losses, they cannot be said to have given an
> example of discipline or military ability to the Spanish troops, nor
> was their achievement greater than that of the Republican army *or at
> least its best fighting units.*[51] [author's emphasis]

The author hopes this volume has made as much clear to the reader: the
International Brigaders were not supermen – but they did fight at the
level of the best units in the People's Army, an army that admittedly set a
low bar as far as military efficiency is concerned. Alongside the crack 11th
and 46th Divisions, the International units were undoubtedly among the
best troops the Republic had at their disposal, or they simply would not
have been used in the way they were.

The military history of the International Brigades is therefore marked
by idealism and incompetence in equal measure. Both these features can
be seen most vividly in the initial phase of the Brigades' existence, during
the battles of the winter of 1936/7 in and around Madrid. At first, the
Internationals resembled only a foreign militia, and training and equipment were rudimentary in the extreme, although it must be said they
compared favourably to those of the peasant and worker militias who had
defended the Republic in the war's first months. From the spring of 1937,
for around a year, the International Brigades were the shock troops of the
new People's Army. Being tried and tested in battle, unlike most units at
the Republic's disposal, they were repeatedly used as the tip of the spear in
a series of bloody offensives. Although training and weaponry had been
improved and standardised to a much greater extent by this period, the
combat performance of the Brigades as shock troops was decidedly mixed,

with heavy losses taking their toll on morale and diluting the ideological commitment of the men through the integration of Spanish conscripts. After the virtual destruction of the International units in the Great Retreats, the Brigades changed once again. They were now effectively foreign-led rather than being a foreign legion, with newly recruited Spaniards rapidly refilling the ranks and grizzled Brigade veterans in officer and NCO positions. The bloodletting did not cease, however, with the Internationals fighting in the toughest spots right up to the announcement of their withdrawal. The combat history of the International Brigades is therefore a story of decline from their first and finest hour in defence of Madrid. The exceptions are the 11th Brigade, which managed to maintain a high level of performance up to the Ebro, and the 15th, which probably peaked in the Belchite campaign of the late summer of 1937. Different Brigades reached the limit of their endurance at different points, but under the astute leadership of General Walter the 11th and 15th Brigades remained effective the longest. As we have seen, a definitive final casualty figure for killed, wounded, captured and missing is impossible to calculate, but likely stands at between 11,000 and 15,000 Internationals. The wearing out of shock units is not a phenomenon exclusive to the International Brigades and was the natural consequence of the tough assignments they were given, rather than being a result of political repression or overly harsh discipline. On Franco's side the Foreign Legion suffered casualties at a remarkably similar level: 7,645 killed and 29,000 wounded, while the *Regulares* lost 11,500 killed, with overall casualties standing at 67,000 of the nearly 80,000 Moroccans who served. The Navarrese Corps, like the Internationals driven by an ideological commitment to the cause but lacking modern tactics and training, numbered just 23,000 at the end of the conflict, from an original strength of 42,000, despite a constant stream of replacements. The elite 13th Black Hand Division of Foreign Legionnaires and Moroccan troops, as we have seen, had to be withdrawn during the Ebro campaign, having suffered nearly 6,500 casualties in the battle. In all these elite Rebel units, the high rate of losses, especially of veteran cadres, resulted in a severe decline in the quality of these crack troops, so that by 1938 they were, on the whole, made up of men just as inexperienced as those in the regular Nationalist divisions, albeit led by a core of veteran soldiers and officers. One can look elsewhere in military history for similar instances. The Australian Imperial Force (more often referred to as the Australian Corps) had a reputation as the most hard-fighting and tenacious unit on the First World War's Western Front and was used time and again by British commanders to spearhead offensives from 1916 onwards. The infantry of this volunteer force suffered a 79 per cent casualty rate over the course of the war, but unlike the Internationals they had the advantage of being at least as well trained and equipped as their German opponents. By September 1918 their combat performance had faded badly, and they were withdrawn from front-line service until the armistice.

There can be little doubt that an International Brigade was of higher combat value than the average mixed brigade of the People's Army. Most of the 150 or so mixed brigades that made up the Republican forces were conscript-heavy and in fact were barely trained units capable of little else than holding the line. This was evidenced in the numerous ill-fated attacks carried out on quiet fronts by virtually static battalions, none of which achieved a significant breakthrough, despite the amateurish nature of the Spanish Civil War trench systems. These brigades were not even capable of the 'active defence' of raid and counter-raid common in the First World War, and, as James Matthews has noted, for most People's Army troops on these static fronts the daily troubles of keeping warm, dry and well fed were greater concerns than any danger in combat, which seldom took place save the exchange of a few shells or pot shots. Some 1.7 million men were theoretically called up by the People's Army (draft dodging was rife, so the figure is certainly inflated) while 1.26 million were conscripted by Franco. Most Spanish men did not wish to fight for either side, while many ended up enlisted by the faction they did not support due to vagaries of geography. The motivation to kill one's countrymen in civil strife was evidently low for these 'reluctant warriors', as Matthews termed them. Remarkably low figures of just 120,000 Spaniards volunteered to fight for the Republic and only 100,000 for the Nationalists. The fact that 32,000 foreigners volunteered for the International Brigades is therefore rather startling. These figures put into context why the International Brigades truly were the shock troops of the People's Army. They represented a huge proportion of the fighting men who were actually committed to the Republican cause. They had sacrificed a great deal just to make it to Spain, and were, for the most part, ideologically driven. Little wonder then that the Republican high command repeatedly placed their trust for major operations not in local formations but in an 'Army of Manoeuvre' that moved from front to front and was made up of the tried and tested veterans of volunteer formations such as the 11th and 46th Divisions, and of course the Internationals. Not all Internationalists fought well all of the time, and some Brigades performed better than others. The 14th's record was dire, while the 12th was excellent in the Madrid battles but its effectiveness quickly waned during 1937. The 11th and 15th Brigades were most consistent in being generally tough, hard-fighting and reliable for the duration of the war, and, once reconstituted with Slavic units, the same could be said of the 13th. Without doubt, in every major battle Spaniards outnumbered Internationals; it cannot be claimed for instance that the International Brigades 'saved Madrid' when they constituted a minority of its defenders. However, the Brigades were repeatedly trusted to hold the critical points of the line or to spearhead attacks on the toughest objectives. No Spanish conscript unit could have stormed Quinto, Purburrel Hill and Belchite in little over a week. It has been asserted that the Internationals were only used as shock troops because of their propaganda value, and that they were in fact no better, or by some accounts were worse, than Spanish formations. Yet the men who devised and planned the Republic's operations, men such as Chief of the General Staff General Rojo and Defence Minister Indalecio Prieto, were not Communists, nor Moscow appointees, and were fighting a bitter civil war for the future of their country. They were not interested in Comintern propaganda. Even the Communist commanders, both Spaniards like Modesto and Red Army personnel such as Walter and Kléber, while loyal to the party, were sincerely trying to win the war, in which case assigning inadequate troops to the most important tasks would have made little sense. The idea that any of these men would subordinate the future of Spain to sympathetic news coverage or party propaganda is both irrational and without foundation in the sources. It seems far more likely, given the generally poor fighting qualities of the People's Army, that the International Brigades were used as shock troops because that is what they were: ideologically committed soldiers, 'commissar material', men who would fight and die in huge numbers whether in suicidal attacks or desperate defence. Perhaps the best evidence for the volunteers' fighting quality, and a point often missed by Brigade critics, is that the Internationals proved on multiple occasions to be a match for the finest units in Franco's army: the Foreign Legion, the Navarrese and the *Regulares* – and as we have seen, the Rebel shock troops suffered similar casualty rates despite superior command and training. Many Brigaders could not cope with the relentless strain; from the University City battles of November and December 1936, through the fighting at Boadilla and the Corunna Road for the following two months, the bloody Jarama battle of February

1937, then the triumph at Guadalajara in March, the first five months of the Brigades' existence consisted of unrelenting combat and slaughter. And that did not change: there followed the botched Segovia and Huesca offensives of May and June, the furnace of Brunete in July, and the Saragossa operation, including the Belchite and Fuentes battles from August to October – a spell which included some of the most intense combat of the war. In January and February 1938 the Brigades were fighting on the Teruel front, before the demoralising retreats of March and April in which so many leaders and veterans were lost. After a much-needed rest, they were back into the vanguard for the great Ebro offensive of July 1938, with constant fighting in the Sierra de Pàndols through August, down to the last stand in September. From start to finish the volunteers were in the heart of the fire, and all the while the Nationalist enemy was growing stronger; from fielding 10,000 men to storm Madrid in 1936 with just a few dozen guns and tanks, they were able to deploy armies of over 160,000 men with dozens of gun batteries and overwhelming air power for the Aragon and Ebro campaigns in 1938. Serving in the International Brigades was a hellish experience because of the high risk of death or injury, the inadequate training and equipment, the lack of home leave and the harsh discipline meted out to those who stepped out of line. Little wonder that so many Brigaders, whether Spanish or International, became demoralised or even looked for a way out of the suicidal assignments they were given in a war that seemed increasingly impossible to win. The International Brigades were indeed shock troops, some of the elite of the People's Army, but with that status came the poison chalice of perpetual clashes against a superior foe and, consequently, murderous casualties. Despite it all, they fought and died for Spain and on the whole fought remarkably well. This is how the International Brigades should be remembered – as ideologically committed soldiers who made up for a lack of training and equipment with heroism and a readiness to sacrifice.

Units of the International Brigades

Brigade	Main Nationalities	Founded	Fate
11th 'Thälmann'	German, Austrian, French, Polish, Dutch, Scandinavian	22 Oct 1936	Initially made up of Germans, French and Polish, reorganised with entirely Germanic volunteers in spring 1937. Repatriated winter 1938.
12th 'Garibaldi'	Italian, German, French, Belgian, Polish, Spanish	5 Nov 1936	Had German and Polish battalions for a time, reorganised with Italian and Spanish units in spring 1937. Repatriated winter 1938.
13th 'Dombrowski'*	Polish, French, Yugoslav, Hungarian, Czech, Swiss	2 Dec 1936	Dissolved and reconstituted July–August 1937 after the Battle of Brunete, Francophone troops moved to 14th Brigade, became a solely Slavic unit. Repatriated winter 1938.
14th 'La Marseillaise'	French, Belgian, British, Spanish	2 Dec 1936	French–Belgian brigade, originally had a British unit which was transferred upon foundation of the 15th Brigade. Repatriated winter 1938.
15th	American, British, Canadian, Irish, Bulgarian, Commonwealth	31 Jan 1937	Anglophone brigade save the presence of Balkan volunteers up to September 1937. Repatriated winter 1938.
129th	Yugoslav, Czech, Bulgarian, German, Greek	13 Feb 1938	Eastern European volunteers separated from other Internationals shortly after formation by Great Retreats. Repatriated winter 1938.
150th	Hungarian, Polish, Yugoslav, Bulgarian, French, Belgian	27 May 1937	Short-lived unit, dissolved July–August 1937 after the Battle of Brunete, Francophone troops to the 14th Brigade, remainder to the 13th

* 'Dabrowski' is the correct Polish spelling but 'Dombrowski' was used in Spain.

Battalion	Main Nationalities	Founded	Brigades served in	Fate
Edgar André	German, Austrian, Dutch, Scandinavian	Oct 1936	11th	Repatriated winter 1938.
Commune de Paris	French, Belgian	Oct 1936	11th, 14th	Repatriated winter 1938.
Garibaldi	Italian, Albanian	Oct 1936	12th	Repatriated winter 1938.
Dombrowski*	Polish, various other Eastern Europeans	Oct 1936	11th, 12th, 150th, 13th	Repatriated winter 1938.
Thälmann	German, Austrian, Scandinavian, British	Oct 1936	12th, 11th	Repatriated winter 1938.
André Marty	French, Belgian, British	Oct 1936	12th, 14th	Repatriated winter 1938.
Louise Michel	French, Belgian	Nov 1936	13th	Merged with Henri Vuillemin battalion in January 1937.
Chapayev	German, Austrian, Swiss, Polish and various others (referred to as the '21-nation battalion')	Dec 1936	13th	Virtually wiped out at the Battle of Brunete in July 1937, dissolved August and troops redistributed to other units in the Brigade.
Nine Nations	French, Belgian, others?	Dec 1936	14th	Presumably dissolved at some point in 1937.
Henri Vuillemin	French	Dec 1936	13th, 14th	Dissolved after the Great Retreats in April 1938, troops redistributed to other units in the 14th Brigade.
Domingo Germinal	French, Spanish	Dec 1936	14th	Merged with Vaillant-Couturier in early 1937.
La Marseillaise (later Ralph Fox)	French, British	Dec 1936	14th	Renamed the Ralph Fox battalion in May 1937 after their deceased British commissar. Dissolved in February 1938 and troops redistributed to other units in the 14th Brigade.
Henri Barbusse	French	Dec 1936	14th	Repatriated winter 1938.
Pierre Brachet	Belgian	Dec 1936	14th	Unknown, likely dissolved in early 1937.
6th February	French, Belgian, North Africans	Dec 1936	15th, 14th	Dissolved after the Great Retreats in April 1938 and troops redistributed to other units in the 14th Brigade.

Battalion	Nationalities	Date	Brigade	Fate
British	British, Irish, Commonwealth	Jan 1937	15th	Repatriated winter 1938.
Abraham Lincoln	American, Irish, Cuban, Canadian	Jan 1937	15th	Repatriated winter 1938.
Dimitrov	Bulgarian, Yugoslav, Greek, German	Dec 1936	15th, 129th	Repatriated winter 1938.
12th February	Austrian, German	Jun 1937	11th	Repatriated winter 1938.
George Washington	American, Canadian	Jun 1937	15th	Merged with Abraham Lincoln battalion during the Battle of Brunete (July 1937) to form the Lincoln-Washingtons.
Rakosi	Hungarian	Apr 1937	150th, 13th	Repatriated winter 1938.
Mackenzie-Papineau	Canadian, American	Jun 1937	15th	Repatriated winter 1938.
Palafox	Polish, Hungarian, Yiddish-speaking Jews, Spanish	Jun 1937	150th, 13th	Repatriated winter 1938.
Adam Mickiewicz	Polish	Oct 1937	13th	Repatriated winter 1938.
Thomas Mazaryck	Czech, Yugoslav	Feb 1938	129th	Repatriated winter 1938.
Duro Daković	Yugoslav, Bulgarian	Jun 1937	150th, 13th, 129th	Repatriated winter 1938.
Vaillant-Couturier	French, Belgian	Dec 1936	14th	Repatriated winter 1938.
Hans Beimler	German, Scandinavian	Mar 1937	11th	Repatriated winter 1938.
Italo-Spanish	Italian, Spanish	Apr 1937	12th	Repatriated winter 1938.
Figlio	Italian, Spanish	Apr 1937	12th	Repatriated winter 1938.

Author's note: units are listed as they were numbered, rather than chronologically. Numerous Spanish battalions that served in the International Brigades at various times are not included. Additionally, a handful of small or especially short-lived International units have also been omitted. The main nationalities are exactly that, the largest groups within each unit. In reality, each International unit contained a greater variety of national groups than is suggested here, as well as having increasingly large complements of Spaniards.

* 'Dabrowski' is the correct Polish spelling but 'Dombrowski' was used in Spain.

Notes

1. Matthews, 1938, pp. 258–9.
2. Matthews, 1938, pp. 261–2.
3. Quoted in Darman, 2009, pp. 23–4.
4. Quoted in Corkill & Rawnsley (eds), 1981, p. 106.
5. Bessie, 1977, p. 46.
6. Voros, 1961, pp. 342–3.
7. Wintringham, 2011, p. 55.
8. Document 70, Radosh *et al.* (eds), 2001, pp. 455–7.
9. Romilly, 2018, pp. 70–1.
10. Document 73, Radosh *et al.* (eds), pp. 465–6.
11. Bessie, pp. 46–7.
12. Whitaker, 1943, p. 100.
13. Sommerfield, 1937, p. 84.
14. Ibid, p. 142.
15. Document 60, Radosh *et al.* (eds), p. 308.
16. Romilly, p. 119.
17. Regler, 1959, p. 284.
18. Ryan (ed.), 2003, p. 45.
19. Ibid, p. 74.
20. Matthews, 1938, pp. 258–9.
21. Matthews, 1938, pp. 261–2.
22. Regler, p. 312.
23. Quoted in Watson & Corcoran, 1996, p. 59.
24. Document 60, Radosh *et al.* (eds), p. 339.
25. Document 49, Radosh *et al.* (eds), pp. 245–6.
26. Ibid, p. 247.
27. Document 60, Radosh *et al.* (eds), p. 356.
28. Ryan (ed.), pp. 255–6.
29. Quoted in Cortada (ed.), 2012, p. 193.
30. Quoted in Carroll, 1994, p. 156.
31. Ryan (ed.), p. 281.
32. Quoted in Cortada (ed.), p. 195.
33. Document 70, Radosh *et al.* (eds), p. 444.
34. Quoted in Cortada (ed.), p. 188.
35. Document 70, Radosh *et al.* (eds), pp. 446–7.
36. Ibid, p. 459.
37. Clark, 1984, pp. 51–2.
38. Ibid, p. 81.
39. Bessie, p. 70.
40. Gregory, 1986, pp. 108–9.
41. Bessie, pp. 124–5, 128.
42. Thomas, 1996, p. 119.
43. Gregory, pp. 125–6.
44. Wheeler, 2003, pp. 76–7.
45. Gregory, p. 129.
46. Bessie, p. 278.
47. Quoted in Henry, 1999, pp. 67–8.
48. Gregory, p. 132.
49. Wolff, 2001, p. 371.
50. Cooney, 2015, p. 106.
51. Thomas, p. 164.
52. Bessie, p. 314.
53. Alpert, 2018, p. 224.

Bibliography

This study has used numerous memoirs and novels by International Brigade and civil war veterans to provide combat detail and character sketches. Of particular use for the training, equipment, discipline and organisation of the Brigades were the accounts of Bessie, Wolff, Wintringham and Copeman. All official Soviet and Comintern reports are taken from Radosh et al's *Spain Betrayed*, the American reports from Cortada's compilation. For the story of British, American and Canadian volunteers I used the excellent national studies of Baxell, Hopkins, Eby, Landis, Carroll and Petrou among others. For other national groups I relied primarily on three older general studies of the IBs (Castells, Brome, Johnston) as well as the first hand accounts of Herbert Matthews and Gustav Regler. The Spanish-language military histories of Hurtado and Cardona were also very useful in this regard. Statistics for troop numbers and casualties are mostly drawn from Hooton, as is the final figure in the conclusion for total IB losses. Otherwise, the figures are taken from my previous study of several key battles, *The People's Army in the Spanish Civil War*. To find my sources for the overall military history of the conflict and the Republican and Francoist armies, including the Spanish primary and secondary material used, see the notes and bibliography of *The People's Army in the Spanish Civil War*.

Primary Sources

Bessie, Alvah, *Men in Battle* (Pinnacle Books, 1977).

Blásquez, José Martin, *I Helped to Build an Army, Civil War Memoirs of a Spanish Staff Officer* (Secker & Warburg, 1939).

Buckley, Henry, *The Life and Death of the Spanish Republic, A Witness to the Spanish Civil War* (I.B. Tauris, 2014).

Cardozo, Harold G., *The March of a Nation, My Year of Spain's Civil War* (Right Book Club, 1937).

Casado, Segismundo, *The Last Days of Madrid* (Peter Davies, 1939).

Clark, Bob, *No Boots to my Feet, Experiences of a Britisher in Spain, 1937–38* (Student Book-shops Ltd, 1984).

Cooney, Bob, *Proud Journey, a Spanish Civil War memoir* (Marx Memorial Library/Manifesto Press, 2015).

Copeman, Fred, *Reason in Revolt* (Blandford Press, 1948).

Corkill, David and Rawnsley, Stuart (eds), *The Road to Spain: Antifascists at War, 1936–9* (1981).

Cortada, James W. (ed.), *Modern Warfare in Spain, American Military Observations on the Spanish Civil War, 1936–1939* (Potomac Books, 2012).

Cox, Geoffrey, *Defence of Madrid: An Eyewitness Account of the Spanish Civil War* (Otago University Press, 2006).

Darman, Peter (ed.), *Heroic Voices of the Spanish Civil War, Memories from the International Brigades* (New Holland, 2009).

Fischer, Louis, *Men and Politics: An Autobiography* (Greenwood Press, 1941).

Gerassi, John, *The Premature Antifascists, North American Volunteers in the Spanish Civil War 1936–1939, An Oral History* (Praeger, 1986).

Gregory, Walter, *The Shallow Grave, A Memoir of the Spanish Civil War* (Gollancz, 1986).

Gurney, Jason, *Crusade in Spain* (Faber, 1974).

Iniesta Cano, Carlos, *Memorias y Recuerdos, Los años que he vivido en el proceso histórico de España* (Planeta, 1984).

Kemp, Peter, *Mine were of Trouble* (Cassell, 1957).

Kindelán, Alfredo, *Mis cuadernos de guerra* (Planeta, 1982).

MacDougall, Ian (ed.), *Voices from the Spanish Civil War: personal recollections of Scottish volunteers in Republican Spain, 1936–39* (Polygon, 1986).

Matthews, Herbert, *Two Wars and More to Come* (Carrick & Evans, 1938).

Max, Jack, *Memorias de un Revolucionario* (Plaza & Janes, 1975).

Merriman, Marion and Lerude, Warren, *American Commander in Spain, Robert Hale Merriman and the Abraham Lincoln Brigade* (University of Nevada Press, 1986).

Modesto, Juan, *Soy del Quinto Regimiento (Notas de la guerra española)* (Colección Ebro, 1974).

Moreno Miranda, Joaquín, extracts from memoirs cited in *El Mundo* (available at: http://www.elmundo.es/cronica/2014/03/30/5336b1beca47418d308b456d.html).

Radosh, Ronald *et al.* (eds), *Spain Betrayed, The Soviet Union in the Spanish Civil War* (Yale University Press, 2001).

Regler, Gustav, *The Owl of Minerva, the Autobiography of Gustav Regler* (Rupert Hart-Davis, 1959).

Revilla Cebrecos, Carmelo, *Tercio de Lácar* (G. Del Toro, 1975).

Rojo, Vicente, *España Heroica, Diez bocetos de la guerra española* (Ariel, 1975).

Romilly, Esmond, *Boadilla* (Clapton Press, 2018).

Rubin, Hank, *Spain's Cause was Mine: A Memoir of an American Medic in the Spanish Civil War* (Southern Illinois University Press, 1997).

Ryan, Frank (ed.), *The Book of the XV Brigade, Records of British, American, Canadian and Irish Volunteers in Spain 1936–1938* (Warren & Pell, 2003).

Sommerfield, John, *Volunteer in Spain* (Lawrence & Wishart, 1937).

Tagüeña Lacorte, Manuel, *Testimonio de dos guerras* (Planeta, 1978).

Thomas, Frank, *Brother against Brother: Experiences of a British Volunteer in the Spanish Civil War* (Sutton, 1998).

Thomas, Fred, *To Tilt at Windmills: A Memoir of the Spanish Civil War* (Michigan State University Press, 1996).

Voros, Sander, *American Commissar* (Chilton, 1961).

Wainwright, John, *The Last to Fall: The Life and Letters of Ivor Hickman – International Brigader* (Open Eye Press, 2014).

Wheeler, George, *To Make the People Smile Again, A Memoir of the Spanish Civil War* (Zymurgy Publishing, 2003).

Whitaker, John T., *We Cannot Escape History* (MacMillan, 1943).

Wintringham, Tom, *English Captain* (Faber, 1939; republished 2011).

Wolff, Milton, *Another Hill* (University of Illinois Press, 2001).

Secondary Sources

Alexander, Bill, *British Volunteers for Liberty: Spain 1936–1939* (Lawrence & Wishart, 1982).

Alpert, Michael, *The Republican Army in the Spanish Civil War, 1936–1939* (Cambridge University Press, 2018).

Balfour, Sebastian, *Deadly Embrace: Morocco and the Road to the Spanish Civil War* (Oxford University Press, 2002).

Baxell, Richard, *British Volunteers in the Spanish Civil War, The British Battalion in the International Brigades, 1936–1939* (Warren & Pell, 2007).

Baxell, Richard, *Unlikely Warriors, The British in the Spanish Civil War and the Struggle Against Fascism* (Aurum Press, 2014).

Baxell, Richard, 'Myths of the International Brigades', *Bulletin of Spanish Studies: Hispanic Studies and Researches on Spain, Portugal and Latin America*, 2014, 91(1–2): 11–24.

Beevor, Antony, *The Battle for Spain, The Spanish Civil War 1936–1939* (Phoenix, 2007).

Blinkhorn, Martin, *Carlism and Crisis in Spain, 1931–1939* (Cambridge University Press, 1975).

Bradley, Ken, *International Brigades in Spain, 1936–39* (Osprey, 1994).

Brome, Vincent, *The International Brigades: Spain, 1936–1939* (Heinemann, 1965).

Cardona, Gabriel, *Historia militar de una guerra civil: estrategias y tácticas de la guerra de España* (Flor del Viento Ediciones, 2006).

Carroll, Peter, *The Odyssey of the Abraham Lincoln Brigade, Americans in the Spanish Civil War* (Stanford University Press, 1994).

Castells, Andreu, *Las brigadas internacionales en la guerra de España* (Editorial Ariel, 1974).

Clifford, Alexander, *The People's Army in the Spanish Civil War, A Military History of the Republic and International Brigades, 1936–1939* (Pen & Sword, 2020).

Collum, Danny (ed.), *African Americans in the Spanish Civil War: 'This Ain't Ethiopia, But It'll Do'* (GK Hall & Co., 1992).

Eby, Cecil D., *Comrades and Commissars: the Lincoln Battalion in the Spanish Civil War* (Pennsylvania State University Press, 2007).

Esdaile, Charles J., *The Spanish Civil War, A Military History* (Routledge, 2018).

Esenwein, George, 'Freedom Fighters or Comintern Soldiers: Writing about the Good Fight during the Spanish Civil War', *Civil Wars*, 2010, 12(1–2): 156–66.

Garcia, Daniel Pastor and Celada, Antonio R., 'The Victors Write History, the Vanquished Literature: Myth, Distortion and Truth in the XV Brigade', *Bulletin of Spanish Studies*, 2012, 89: 7–8.

Graham, Helen, *The Spanish Republic at War, 1936–1939* (Cambridge University Press, 2002).

Gray, Daniel, *Homage to Caledonia: Scotland and the Spanish Civil War* (Luath Press, 2009).

Henry, Chris, *The Ebro 1938, Death Knell of the Republic* (Osprey, 1999).

Hills, George, *The Battle for Madrid* (Vantage Books, 1976).

Hochschild, Adam, *Spain in Our Hearts, Americans in the Spanish Civil War, 1936–1939* (Pan, 2017).

Hooton, E.R., *Spain in Arms: A Military History of the Spanish Civil War, 1936–1939* (Casemate, 2019).

Hopkins, James, *Into the Heart of the Fire: The British in the Spanish Civil War* (Stanford University Press, 1998).

Howson, Gerald, *Arms for Spain, The Untold Story of the Spanish Civil War* (John Murray, 1998).

Hurtado, Víctor, *Las Brigadas Internacionales* (Dau, 2013).

Jensen, Geoffrey, *Irrational Triumph: Cultural Despair, Military Nationalism, and the Ideological Origins of Franco's Spain* (University of Nevada Press, 2002).

Johnston, Verle B., *Legions of Babel: The International Brigades in the Spanish Civil War* (Pennsylvania University Press, 1967).

Keene, Judith, *Fighting for Franco: International Volunteers in Nationalist Spain during the Spanish Civil War, 1936–1939* (Leicester University Press, 2001).

Krammer, Arnold, 'Germans against Hitler: The Thaelmann Brigade', *Journal of Contemporary History*, 1969, 4(2): 65–83.

Landis, Arthur H., *Death in the Olive Groves, American Volunteers in the Spanish Civil War, 1936–1939* (Paragon House, 1989).

Matthews, James, *Reluctant Warriors, Republican Popular Army and Nationalist Army Conscripts in the Spanish Civil War, 1936–1939* (Oxford University Press, 2012).

Payne, Stanley G., *The Spanish Civil War* (Cambridge University Press, 2012).

Petrou, Michael, *Renegades, Canadians in the Spanish Civil War* (Warren & Pell, 2008).

Preston, Paul, *Franco, A Biography* (Fontana, 1995).

Preston, Paul, *The Spanish Civil War, Reaction, Revolution and Revenge* (Harper Perennial, 2006).

Quesada, Alejandro de, *The Spanish Civil War 1936–39 (1), Nationalist Forces* (Osprey, 2014).

Quesada, Alejandro de, *The Spanish Civil War 1936–39 (2), Republican Forces* (Osprey, 2015).

Richardson, Dan R., *Comintern Army: The International Brigades and the Spanish Civil War* (University Press of Kentucky, 1982).

Seidmann, Michael, *The Victorious Counter-Revolution, The Nationalist Effort in the Spanish Civil War* (University of Wisconsin Press, 2011).

Smyth, Denis, '"We are with you": Solidarity and Self-interest in Soviet Policy towards Republican Spain, 1936–1939', in Preston & Mackenzie (eds.), *The Republic Besieged: Civil War in Spain 1936–1939* (Edinburgh University Press, 1996).

Stradling, Robert, *The Irish and the Spanish Civil War, 1936–39* (Mandolin, 1999).

Thomas, Hugh, *The Spanish Civil War, Fourth Edition* (Penguin, 2012).

Watson, Don and Corcoran, John, *An Inspiring Example: The North East of England and the Spanish Civil War, 1936–1939* (McGuffin Press, 1996).

Zaloga, Steven J., *Spanish Civil War Tanks, The Proving Ground for Blitzkrieg* (Osprey, 2010).

Index